Walking and Running
The Complete Guide

Fitness, Health & Nutrition was created by Rebus, Inc. and published by Time-Life Books.

REBUS, INC.

Publisher: RODNEY FRIEDMAN
Editorial Director: CHARLES L. MEE JR.

Editor: THOMAS DICKEY
Senior Editor: WILLIAM DUNNETT
Text Editor: LINDA EPSTEIN
Associate Editor: MARY CROWLEY
Chief of Research: CARNEY W. MIMMS III
Copy Editor: ROBERT HERNANDEZ
Contributing Editors: JACQUELINE DAMIAN, JANE SCHECHTER

Art Director: JUDITH HENRY
Associate Art Director: FRANCINE KASS
Designer: SARA BOWMAN
Still Life and Food Photographer: STEVEN MAYS
Contributing Photographer: DAVID MADISON
Photo Stylist: LEAH LOCOCO

Test Kitchen Director: GRACE YOUNG
Recipe Editor: BONNIE J. SLOTNICK

Time-Life Books Inc. is a wholly owned subsidiary of

TIME INCORPORATED

Founder: HENRY R. LUCE 1898-1967

Editor-in-Chief: JASON McMANUS
Chairman and Chief Executive Officer: J. RICHARD MUNRO
President and Chief Operating Officer: N.J. NICHOLAS JR.
Corporate Editor: RICHARD B. STOLLEY
Executive Vice President, Books: KELSO F. SUTTON
Vice President, Books: PAUL V. McLAUGHLIN

TIME-LIFE BOOKS INC.

Editor: GEORGE CONSTABLE

Executive Editor: ELLEN PHILLIPS
Director of Design: LOUIS KLEIN
Director of Editorial Resources: PHYLLIS K. WISE
Editorial Board: RUSSELL B. ADAMS JR., DALE M. BROWN, ROBERTA CONLAN, THOMAS H. FLAHERTY, LEE HASSIG, DONIA ANN STEELE, ROSALIND STUBENBERG
Director of Photography and Research: JOHN CONRAD WEISER
Assistant Director of Editorial Resources: ELISE RITTER GIBSON

President: CHRISTOPHER T. LINEN
Chief Operating Officer: JOHN M. FAHEY JR.
Senior Vice Presidents: ROBERT M. DeSENA, JAMES L. MERCER, PAUL R. STEWART
Vice Presidents: STEPHEN L. BAIR, RALPH J. CUOMO, NEAL GOFF, STEPHEN L. GOLDSTEIN, JUANITA T. JAMES, CAROL KAPLAN, SUSAN J. MARUYAMA, ROBERT H. SMITH, JOSEPH J. WARD
Director of Production Services: ROBERT J. PASSANTINO
Supervisor of Quality Control: JAMES KING

FITNESS, HEALTH & NUTRITION

Walking and Running
The Complete Guide

Time-Life Books, Alexandria, Virginia

CONSULTANTS FOR THIS BOOK

Marshall Clark is the Assistant Athletic Director at San Jose State University in California and head coach of the track and field team. He has also coached track and field at the University of Montana and Stanford University, and has trained United States Olympians in the 5,000-meter race and the marathon.

Wayne Glusker is a member of the Athletics Congress Race Walk development committee. He is a former 35-kilometer national champion and has been a member of the United States track and field team. Glusker lives in San Jose, California, where he coaches race walking.

William D. McArdle, Ph.D., is a professor in the Department of Health and Physical Education at Queens College of the City University of New York. A Fellow of the American College of Sports Medicine, he is the author of *Exercise Physiology: Energy, Nutrition, and Human Performance; Getting in Shape* and *Nutrition, Weight Control, and Exercise.*

Michael A. Motta, M.A., is the chief executive officer of Plus One, a fitness clinic in New York City. He has completed work leading to a doctorate of education in exercise physiology, and he has taught physical education and served as a coach at the State University of New York at Albany.

Allan J. Ryan, M.D., is the editor-in-chief of *Fitness in Business* magazine and the former editor-in-chief of *The Physician and Sportsmedicine* and *Postgraduate Medicine.* He is a former president of the American College of Sports Medicine and a member of many sports medicine and orthopedic organizations.

Bruce Wolfe is a member of the United States orienteering team. He is president of the Bay Area Orienteering Club and has taught orienteering at the University of California at Berkeley, at American River College in Sacramento and to such groups as the Sierra Club and the Boy Scouts.

Nutritional Consultants

Ann Grandjean, Ed.D., is Associate Director of the Swanson Center for Nutrition, Omaha, Neb.; chief nutrition consultant to the U.S. Olympic Committee; and an instructor in the Sports Medicine Program, Orthopedic Surgery Department, University of Nebraska Medical Center.

Myron Winick, M.D., is the R.R. Williams Professor of Nutrition, Professor of Pediatrics, Director of the Institute of Human Nutrition, and Director of the Center for Nutrition, Genetics and Human Development at Columbia University College of Physicians and Surgeons. He has served on the Food and Nutrition Board of the National Academy of Sciences and is the author of many books, including *Your Personalized Health Profile.*

For information about any Time-Life book please call 1-800-621-7026, or write:
Reader Information
Time-Life Customer Service
P.O. Box C-32068
Richmond, Virginia 23261-2068

First printing.
Published simultaneously in Canada.
School and library distribution by Silver Burdett Company, Morristown, New Jersey.

TIME-LIFE is a trademark of Time Incorporated U.S.A.

Library of Congress Cataloging-in-Publication Data
Walking and running: a complete guide.
    p. cm. — (Fitness, health & nutrition)
    Includes index.
    ISBN 0-8094-6130-7
    ISBN 0-8094-6131-5 (lib. bdg.)
    1. Walking—Health aspects. 2. Running—Health aspects. I. Time-Life Books. II Series: Fitness, health, and nutrition.
    RA781.65.W35   1989   88-38930
    613.7'1—dc19   CIP

This book is not intended as a substitute for the advice of a physician or an athletic coach. Readers who have or suspect they may have specific medical problems should consult a physician before beginning any program of strenuous physical exercise.

CONTENTS

CHAPTER ONE

The Premier Exercises

Varied, convenient, suitable for virtually anyone — and with a multitude of benefits

As forms of exercise, walking and running are no longer fads: Millions of people have discovered the physical and psychological dividends of these two activities and have made them a permanent part of their lives. It is not difficult to understand why: Both exercises are suitable for any age, they can be performed alone or in a group, they require no special skills, and you need not join a club, use machinery or purchase special equipment (other than proper shoes) to enjoy them. You can step out the front door and take off. For people who have never undertaken an exercise program, walking and running are excellent ways to get started — and this book will show you the safest, most effective ways to design a program for either exercise. If you already walk or run, you will find information to help you hone your technique, upgrade your program and, most important, add variety to keep your regimen invigorating mentally and physically. The specific fitness benefits of walking and running are spelled out in this chapter.

Why are walking and running such good exercises?

Both effectively develop cardiovascular endurance — the most important component of overall fitness — because they are aerobic exercises, meaning that they develop the heart's capacity to deliver oxygenated blood to the working muscles and simultaneously improve their capacity to use this oxygen. Aerobic exercise requires continuous, rhythmical movement of at least 50 percent of your body's muscle mass. To condition your heart effectively, that exercise must raise your heart rate above 65 percent of its maximum capacity for at least 20 minutes. Walking and running use all the major muscles in your legs, which comprise about four times the muscle mass of your arms. When these muscles work, they require oxygen from the blood, which makes your heart pump faster to deliver that blood. Like any other muscle, the heart becomes stronger in response to having to work harder, and the more powerful your heart, the more blood it pumps per beat; consequently, the less often it has to pump to deliver blood to your muscles.

Many benefits are attributed to regular aerobic exercise. The most important result is reducing the risk of cardiovascular disease, the leading cause of mortality in the United States. Regular exercise has been shown to increase the pumping capacity of the heart and possibly the diameter of coronary arteries, while also lowering the blood concentrations of triglycerides (fatty acids) and low-density lipoproteins, or LDLs, the "bad" cholesterol that causes plaque to accumulate on the walls of arteries. Regular exercise also appears to raise the level of high-density lipoproteins, the "good" HDLs, which carry cholesterol to the liver to be broken down.

Among the other benefits associated with aerobic exercise are a reduction in the risks of osteoporosis, hypertension, diabetes and enhances the ability to maintain optimal body weight. Psychological tests have shown that those who start exercising become more self-confident and emotionally stable. In addition, regular physical activity — even if it is not strenuous enough to raise your heart rate to 65 percent of its maximum — has recently been shown to reduce the risk of stroke, respiratory disease, cancer, and even death.

Are walking and running better for your health than other forms of aerobic exercise?

No. You can derive similar fitness and health benefits by cycling, rowing, aerobic dancing, jumping rope, swimming, cross-country skiing and any other activity in which you move the large skeletal muscles, especially the leg muscles, for a continuous period of time. However, many people find that the activities of walking and running are more convenient than the others because — by their very simplicity and accessibility — they are simple to begin and easy to maintain on a regular basis.

Most people, even those who have been completely sedentary, can walk to improve their fitness. And with a minimum amount of effort

The Biomechanics of Walking and Running

At first glance, the biomechanics of walking and running seem about the same: Each foot alternately stays in contact with the ground and propels your body forward. However, as you move from walking to running, you change the biomechanics of your stride significantly, as shown below.

The walking gait can be divided into two phases: stance and swing. The stance portion consists of the initial foot strike and the movement of the legs to the point where your other foot makes contact with the ground. The swing portion brings your leg back to the original foot strike position.

In running (bottom), the same basic motions make up stance and swing, but the stance phase is shortened because your pace is faster. Also, the moment in the walking cycle when both feet are on the ground is replaced by the float phase, during which the body is propelled through the air.

Walking

STANCE (65%)				SWING (35%)	

Right foot strike — Mid-stance — Toe off — Left foot strike — Mid-stance — Right foot strike

Running

STANCE (40%)		FLOAT (15%)	SWING (30%)		FLOAT (15%)

Right foot strike — Mid-stance — Toe off — Left foot strike — Mid-stance — Right foot strike

Energy for Speed vs. Distance

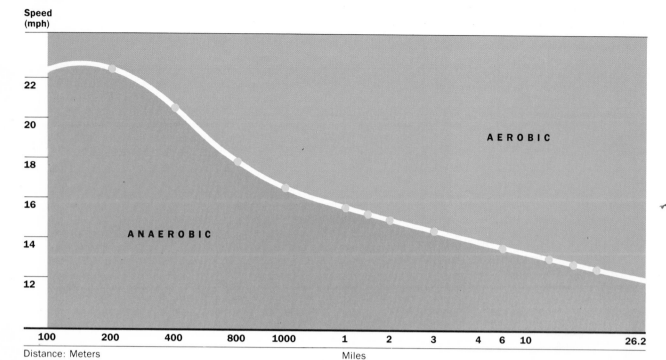

Speed (mph)

AEROBIC

ANAEROBIC

22
20
18
16
14
12

100 200 400 800 1000 1 2 3 4 6 10 26.2

Distance: Meters

Miles

Fuel for exercise is provided by the body's two energy systems: aerobic (meaning "with air") and anaerobic ("without air"). The chart above plots the speeds maintained by elite athletes in a variety of running events, from sprints to the marathon, and the arc of this performance curve suggests the contribution of each energy system. The short, intense sprints at the left are predominantly anaerobic, while the longer endurance runs are mainly aerobic. At the 800- to 1,000-meter zone, each system provides an equal amount of energy. And neither system is ever totally dominant; there is always some contribution, however small, by the other.

and training, most people can also run. To ensure that you will keep exercising throughout your life, experts advise that your workout program be simple: The less organization, equipment, expense or traveling you need to do, the better. In addition, your exercise program should somehow be incorporated into your everyday activities. The less equipment or preparation you need, and the less you depend on going to a class or health club, the better. Recent data suggest that people who engage in informal exercise on their own — like walking and running — are most likely to continue with their training for the long term.

Many experts also believe that a lifetime exercise program should have as much diversity as possible. No routine fulfills this requirement better than walking and running. Both activities can be practiced indoors or outside, and you can vary the kind of walking and running you do — from exercise walking to hiking and orienteering, from race walking and jogging to sprinting, "fun running" (racing without pressuring yourself to win) and competing in a marathon — as this book will show you.

Is running better than walking?

The answer to this question depends on what your goals and preferences are, and which activities best fit into your everyday life. While it may be more difficult to raise your heart rate to your training range

— that is, between 65 and 85 percent of its maximum — by walking, many people find that walking is easier to incorporate into their daily lives. Walking to work, or part way to work, is an option for many people who cannot change their clothes when they arrive, as they would probably need to if they ran to work. According to the Canada Fitness Survey, the convenience of walking has made it the most popular exercise of all.

Because the impact force of running is two to three times body weight — much more than the impact force of walking — runners are somewhat more likely to be injured than walkers, and running can be too stressful for some out-of-shape beginners. However, running is tremendously popular: In the United States, an estimated 25 million people run at least three times per week. Some runners find that competition motivates them to stick with an exercise program, and the existence of numerous races makes them prefer running to walking for their regular workouts.

The question of whether to walk or run is also related to another question: Is cardiovascular fitness your goal, or simply physical activity? Running is a powerful conditioner for the cardiovascular system; for many people, walking is less intense. Experts disagree on which is best for you. However, one major study followed more than 10,000 men for a little longer than eight years and correlated their exercise and activity habits with mortality from all causes. Called the Aerobics Center Longitudinal Study, this research found that both running and walking probably have about equal benefit for increasing your lifespan.

How are fitness and activity measured?

Fitness can be measured by the volume of oxygen you can consume while exercising at your maximum capacity. This is your VO_2max. Those who are more fit have higher VO_2max values and can exercise more intensely than those who are not as well conditioned. Numerous studies show that you can increase your VO_2max by working out at an intensity that will raise your heart rate to a level between 65 and 85 percent of its maximum for at least 20 minutes three to five times a week.

Your activity level is more difficult to measure. Researchers generally must rely on reports submitted by study subjects. In the Harvard Alumni Study of nearly 17,000 male graduates, subjects reported how many city blocks they walked, how many stairs they climbed, the types of sports they engaged in and the time they spent on these activities each week. The researchers assigned energy costs for each activity — 56 calories for walking seven city blocks, for instance, and 28 calories for climbing 70 stairs. Those who were active and burned more calories suffered less from cardiovascular disease and other illnesses than their sedentary peers did; the active ones also tended to live longer. Furthermore, those who expended at least 2,000 calories per week on physical activity had the greatest overall reduction in the risk of death.

How much should you walk or run each week to increase your odds of living longer?

Since you burn approximately 100 calories a mile when you run, you will expend 2,000 calories if you run 20 miles a week, thus putting yourself in the lower risk category for premature death. Most people could cover 20 miles a week if they ran for about 30 to 40 minutes per day for five days. And brisk walking for at least 20 miles per week will also fulfill the requirement for burning 2,000 calories, although this may require walking from five to eight hours per week. Although many people may not be able to accumulate this amount of walking time on a weekly basis, the findings of the Harvard study also showed that simply walking nine miles a week will reduce significantly your chances of developing heart disease.

Is strenuous walking enough to improve fitness?

Many people wonder if walking (other than race walking) is strenuous enough to produce any aerobic benefits or help you lose weight. To test this, researchers at the University of Massachusetts asked 271 males and females aged 30 to 69 to walk as fast as they could on a treadmill for the equivalent of one mile. While the subjects walked, the researchers monitored their heart rates and found that at least 86 percent of all the females, regardless of age, and 81 percent of the males over 50 years old were able to walk vigorously enough to maintain a heart rate of 70 percent of maximum. The researchers found, however, that many of the younger, fitter males were unable to attain their target heart rates, and that for them, walking was not intense enough to ensure an aerobic benefit.

On the other hand, it may not be necessary to exercise at such an intensity that you achieve your target heart rate of 65 to 85 percent of your maximum. (To find your target heart rate, see page 17.) Many benefits attributed to training at high levels of intensity can also be achieved by training at lower levels. Researchers at the University of Pittsburgh asked 10 sedentary men to walk briskly on a treadmill for 20 minutes. They found that this level of exercise, which raised the subjects' heart rates to an average of 50 percent of maximum, raised their blood levels of HDL cholesterol significantly without raising the overall cholesterol level.

In addition, research has shown that lower-intensity exercise will also increase aerobic fitness if the duration of the activity is sufficient. In essence, if the intensity of your exercise session is reduced, lengthen the time you work out.

In any case, there are many ways to make walking intense enough to raise your heart rate into its target zone and to expend enough calories to make you lose weight. These include hill walking, carrying hand weights and race walking (see Chapter Two).

If running is good for you, why are runners injured so often?

While it is true that runners get hurt, their injuries are usually minor.

A few days of rest or cutting back on your mileage or the intensity of your workout generally results in a complete recovery. Some exercise physiologists believe that the risk of injury to runners is exaggerated. They point out that statistics regarding injury rates for runners and others who exercise are often meaningless because the studies fail to use control groups.

In one study that did use a control, researchers asked two groups of individuals — one group that ran and performed other exercises, and the control group that was inactive — whether they had a bone, muscle or joint injury within the past year that caused them to stop exercising or curtail other activities for at least a week. The researchers found only a 10 percent difference in injury rates between the two groups. In another study of 3,000 injured runners and nonrunners who sought medical care, researchers found only a 2 percent difference in injury rates between the two groups. Although the runners had more knee problems than those who did not run, injury rates were similar for both groups for the hip, ankle, foot, back, elbow and shoulder areas.

Are you in danger of a heart attack if you run too hard?

The concern that running can place too much stress on the heart was sparked in 1984 by the death of marathon runner and best-selling author James Fixx, who died of a heart attack while running. A study published in 1987 reported 36 cases of heart attack or sudden death in marathon runners worldwide. These deaths dispelled a widely held notion that anyone fit enough to run a marathon, an extremely demanding 26.2-mile road race, simply could not have life-threatening coronary artery disease.

However, the same study found that 71 percent of the victims had experienced symptoms of cardiovascular disease but had ignored them, just as James Fixx was reported to have done. He had refused to have a complete physical examination or to take a stress test; apparently, so that he was unaware of his condition. Indeed, Fixx had many risk factors that predisposed him to heart disease, and he may have lived an even shorter life had he not been a runner.

In the general population, exercise-related deaths are actually quite rare: One study of active males whose ages ranged from 30 to 64 revealed that the risk of their dropping dead while running was one in 7,620. And although physically active people have a slightly higher chance of dying from a heart attack while they are exercising than when they are not, their overall risk of sudden death is 60 percent less than that of sedentary men.

Among cardiologists and physical therapists, walking and running are now widely accepted as healthful exercises for recovering cardiac patients. As long as patients are carefully monitored and do not have symptoms that indicate a potential problem, they can increase their training. In fact, at least three heart-transplant recipients have completed marathons.

The Training Zone

% VO₂ max

% maximum heart rate

To obtain aerobic benefits from walking and running, you must exercise at your target heart rate, which varies with your age and falls within a zone ranging from 65 to 85 percent of your maximum heart rate. As the chart above shows, this training zone can be correlated to maximum oxygen uptake, or VO₂max, a precise measurement of fitness that expresses the amount of oxygen your body can take in and use during one minute of intense exercise. *(Instructions for determining your target heart rate are given on page 17.)*

How can you keep walking and running from becoming monotonous routines?

About 50 percent of people who are concerned enough with their health to begin exercise programs drop out within six months to a year — even cardiac patients, who stand to benefit the most from exercise, drop out at a rate as high as 70 percent. Studies show that those who withdrew from exercise programs reported that their workout routines were boring or the facilities were expensive and inconvenient. If you walk or run, expense and inconvenience will not be problems; as this book shows, both exercises can be varied sufficiently to help keep your interest and motivation levels from flagging.

A study of 1,299 patients at the Cooper Clinic in Dallas, Texas, is a case in point. It showed that at the first of four clinic visits, only 50 percent of the subjects were active. By the fourth visit, 96 percent of those who were active initially were still exercising. Of those who were inactive initially, 75 percent were exercising by the final visit. Part of the clinic's high success rate may be the result of its repeated testing of patients, which is thought to motivate them to improve their fitness.

As an alternative to motivation provided by a clinic's frequent testing, you may find that competition helps you stick to a training program. Generally speaking, if you train to race, you will be improving your fitness along with your performance. It is not necessary to train at a competitive athlete's level to be fit; you can take advantage of many techniques that athletes use — such as running intervals on a track or "fartlek" training, or "speed play" — to improve your enjoyment of exercise as well as your performance *(see Chapter Three)*. Entering races and fun runs thus becomes a tool for self-evaluation and motivation.

Should you engage in other exercises and activities in addition to walking or running?

There are many aspects of fitness — for instance, strength, speed, endurance, aerobic fitness, coordination, flexibility, balance, agility and the ratio of lean-to-fat body tissue. Walking and running, while they are excellent aerobic and endurance conditioners that also help reduce body fat, may not adequately build all other aspects of fitness with equal effectiveness. Many runners and walkers, therefore, would benefit from flexibility training and upper body workouts to develop strength and upper body muscle endurance.

Both the walking and running chapters *(see Chapters Two and Three)* offer stretching routines to enhance flexibility and joint range of motion. Chapter Four *(see pages 108-123)* gives an upper body strength-training workout designed specifically to condition walkers and runners.

The Training Effect

The first link in the oxygen-delivery system to be affected by exercise is the lungs. When you begin to exercise aerobically, your ventilation increases exponentially for the first several minutes, then settles into a fairly steady elevated state that lasts as long as the activity does.

In fact, the lungs of an untrained person actually deliver more oxygen than his unconditioned skeletal muscles and heart can use. As a result, the heart and other muscles are the limiting factors in performance, as suggested by the illustration above.

Ultimately, though, the situation is reversed *(below)*, since the skeletal muscles and heart make far more significant adaptations to exercise than do the lungs, which are capable of only modest alterations. The most profound changes are in the skeletal muscles; their rich net work of capillaries expands, along with the number of microscopic energy factories called mitochondria. Next is the heart, which pumps more blood. Thus, in a highly fit person, the lungs may be the limiting factor in improved performance.

How to Design Your Own Program

There are three keys to designing a satisfying exercise program: Know what your goals are; choose an activity that you enjoy and can work into your daily schedule; and get started properly. The latter is especially important; studies show that the most common mistake that people make is to start an exercise program too aggressively. If you try to do too much too soon, you are likely to tire quickly, become discouraged and increase your chances of getting injured.

The questions and answers on these two pages will help you evaluate your current level of fitness and your exercise goals; the following five pages show how to develop a walking or running schedule that is comfortable and gradually progressive. This section also contains guidelines for choosing equipment and a chart for preventing injuries.

What shape are you in?

1 How active are you?

Your general level of fitness hinges on three components: how often, how long and how vigorously you perform an activity. To be minimally fit, you should exercise at least three times a week for 20 minutes each time. Equally important, the exercise should raise your pulse and breathing rate for a sustained period— that is, it should be aerobic. Activities that involve bursts of strength or speed — such as weigh lifting or tennis — are predominantly anaerobic, and while they may provide some aerobic benefits, they are not nearly as good for building cardiovascular fitness as walking or running.

2 How fit are your heart and lungs?

The ability of your cardiovascular system to sustain an endurance activity like walking or running is the primary indicator of fitness. The most accurate way to judge this ability is with a laboratory test in which you run on a treadmill or ride a bicycle while your oxygen consumption is measured. Such an exercise stress test usually is not necessary if you are under 35 and in good health. But if moderate activity — for instance, walking up a flight of stairs — makes you winded, then you probably have a low level of cardiovascular endurance. If that is the case, start your exercise program by walking or by following the guidelines for running beginners on pages 20 and 21. If you have not exercised regularly in over a year, if you are over 35, or if you are at any risk of heart disease, you should consult your physician before beginning an exercise program.

3 Are you overweight?

Excessive fat detracts from your appearance and contributes to a variety of health problems, including high cholesterol levels. The extra weight also places a burden on virtually all of the body's organs, especially the heart, as well as on joints and muscles.

Studies have shown that many obese people do not eat significantly more than thin individuals, but are much less active. A crucial part of any weight-loss program, therefore, is adding activities to your daily life that increase calorie expenditure substantially. The charts on pages 19 and 20 show the number of calories you burn while walking and running, and suggest workout guidelines that will allow you to lose significant amounts of fat.

4 Have you ever sustained a stress injury?

Stress injuries are caused by overloading muscles, ligaments and tendons over a period of days or weeks. The damage may have no obvious cause, but it often results in inflammation of the stressed tissues, accompanied by such symptoms as pain or swelling in muscles or tendons, and stiffness or pain in joints. (The chart on pages 22-23 cites the causes of specific injuries.) If you have tried running and given it up because of a stress injury, you can guard against re-injury by wearing proper shoes and building up your training program gradually. (For tips on choosing shoes, see pages 24-25.)

5 Do you want to walk or run?

Theroretically, the most effective exercise is the one that promotes the highest VO$_2$max — the indicator of how efficiently your system processes oxygen for energy. But unless you already train at high intensity, your heart is likely to benefit from walking as well as running. It is most important to choose an activity that is accessible to you and that you enjoy — studies show these two qualities provide the best insurance for sticking with an exercise. If you decide to pursue a walking program, you can use hand weights to increase the intensity of the exercise as your level of fitness improves.. Walkers can also progress to running, while many runners will enjoy the walking variations such as hiking and orienteering covered in Chapter Two.

6 If you already walk or run, do you also perform any other exercises regularly?

While walking and running help build muscular strength and endurance in your lower body, they contribute little to keeping your upper body strong, firm and flexible. Strength and flexibility help you perform all sorts of tasks with greater ease and agility and also reduce your chances of injury to muscles and joints. If you presently do not perform a workout for your upper body, the strengthening exercises in Chapter Four should become an integral part of your weekly exercise regimen.

How hard to train

The pace at which you walk or run is of vital importance to achieve optimal aerobic benefits. Researchers have determined that your heart rate can serve as a guide to exercise intensity, and they have devised a simple formula for figuring the rate that you should aim for during an aerobic workout.

To find your target heart rate, first determine your maximum heart rate, which is 220 minus your age. Multiply that figure first by 65 percent and then by 85 percent. After warming up, your heart rate during exercise should be somewhere between the two numbers you have calculated. If you are 35 years old, for example, your target heart rate should reach at least 120 beats per minute and not exceed 157 beats. Most people will find that after several months, exercising in the 70 to 80 percent range is comfortable.

To find your heart rate while exercising, stop briefly to take your pulse at the main artery in your wrist. Count the number of beats for 10 seconds and multiply by six.

Walking Workouts

To derive aerobic benefits from walking, you need only increase the pace at which you normally walk. Walking at a normal pace is an efficient activity that does not take much energy. As you walk faster, however, you become less efficient and burn more calories.

As the chart opposite shows, oxygen consumption and caloric expenditure rise steadily as you increase your speed from two miles per hour to about four miles per hour. At even faster speeds, the caloric expenditure rises so quickly — in part, because the efficiency of the walking stride starts to decline — that researchers have found it is not possible to predict accurately how many calories you can burn by walking at these speeds.

However, you do not have to walk at top speed to get a good workout. The lower chart on the opposite page shows that swinging your arms vigorously while carrying hand weights can be adequate exercise even at a normal walking speed.

Exercise walking is not the only way to walk for fitness. You can also get a good workout from hiking over rugged terrain, orienteering through the wilderness with a map and compass as your guide or race walking, a competitive sport. The guide below summarizes these forms of walking and refers you to pages that describe them in greater detail.

A Walking Guide

EXERCISE WALKING	ORIENTEERING	HIKING	RACE WALKING
To walk for exercise, use a thrusting stride and vigorous arm swings to increase the number of calories burned. Carry one- to three-pound hand weights to boost the intensity of workouts.	Cross-country hiking using a map and compass is called orienteering. This can be a competitive activity with formal meets and championships, or simply a way to navigate unknown territory.	Hiking means trail walking, often with a backpack. Hiking is most frequently a weekend or vacation activity that can add variety to your regular workout. Its challenges come from difficult terrain.	The fastest, most energetic form of walking is race walking. A competitive sport and an Olympic event, race walking is an excellent fitness-building activity and can be an aid in weight control.
Pages 38-45.	Pages 54-59.	Pages 52-53.	Pages 46-51.

Calories Burned by Walking

MPH	BODY WEIGHT IN LBS.				
	120	140	160	180	200
2.0	2.6	2.9	3.2	3.5	3.8
2.5	3.1	3.5	3.8	4.2	4.5
3.0	3.6	4.0	4.4	4.8	5.3
3.5	4.2	4.6	5.0	5.4	6.1
4.0	4.7	5.2	5.8	6.4	7.0

Approximate caloric expenditure per minute based on walking speed and body weight.

Increasing the Effort

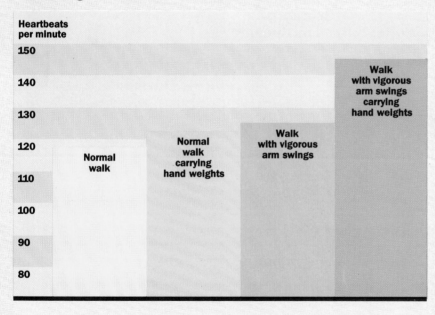

The chart at left compares ways in which you can increase the intensity of walking. Based on a study of college students, it shows that either carrying three-pound hand weights or swinging your arms vigorously will probably only elevate your heart rate slightly. However, the subjects who carried hand weights and swung their arms vigorously at the same time raised their heart rates by over 20 percent.

Running Workouts

First and foremost, running should be fun. If you run to fulfill someone else's notion of what you should be doing, you will not enjoy it. The charts on the opposite page give three sample running schedules; however, you need not adhere to them strictly. Instead, use them as guidelines.

If you are just starting out as a runner, begin by jogging two or three times a week for 10 to 15 minutes. Do not worry about the distance you run; work on increasing your time gradually, building up to four days a week. Pick one day on the weekend to put in a longer run.

Once you have established a beginning schedule and have maintained it for a month or more, graduate to an intermediate level such as the one shown on the opposite page. Increase your training program until you run six days a week for at least 30 minutes a day, with an hour run on the weekend.

If you want to begin training on a more advanced level, start running for distance. Measure the length of specific routes in your car. Take easy runs of five miles and up, and harder runs for shorter distances, on alternate days of the week. Do a long run on the weekend and be sure to take one day off, as the chart at bottom right shows. The chart below tells how many calories you burn by running at various speeds.

Calories Burned by Running

MPH	BODY WEIGHT IN LBS.				
	120	140	160	180	200
5.0	7.1	8.3	9.4	10.7	11.8
5.5	7.8	9.0	10.4	11.7	13.0
6.0	9.4	11.0	12.5	14.0	15.7
6.5	10.1	11.9	13.6	15.2	17.0
7.0	10.9	12.9	14.6	16.4	18.2
7.5	11.6	13.4	15.2	16.8	18.6
8.0	12.1	13.8	15.3	16.9	18.7
8.5	12.8	14.6	16.3	18.0	19.9
9.0	13.6	15.5	17.3	19.0	21.0
9.5	14.4	16.4	18.3	20.0	22.2
10.0	15.7	16.5	17.3	19.9	21.7

Approximate caloric expenditure per minute based on running speed and body weight.

Sample Workouts

GETTING STARTED
Running continuously without regard for speed

M	Tu	W	Th	F	Sa	Su
20 min.	OFF	20 min.	OFF	20 min.	OFF	30 min.

INTERMEDIATE SCHEDULE
Running continuously at 6-8 mph

M	Tu	W	Th	F	Sa	Su
30 min.	30 min.	30 min.	30 min.	45 min.	OFF	60 min.

PRECOMPETITIVE SCHEDULE
Varying workout intensity on alternate days

M	Tu	W	Th	F	Sa	Su
3-5 mi. HARD	5 mi. EASY	3-5 mi. HARD	5 mi. EASY	3-5 mi. HARD	OFF	8-10 mi. EASY

HARD: A pace that works your heart at 75-85 percent of your maximum heart rate.
EASY: A pace that works your heart at 60-75 percent of your maximum heart rate.

Common Running and Walking Complaints

Most runners and many walkers occasionally experience discomfort or pain due to injury. Many of these are stress, or overuse, injuries, the result of repeated microtrauma caused by intensive running and walking. If you are injured, cut back on your training or stop altogether. Ice the affected area and keep it elevated for as long as you experience pain and swelling. If pain persists, or if you have any questions about your injury, consult a physician.

COMPLAINT/SYMPTOMS	PREVENTION AND RECOVERY TIPS
Achilles tendinitis Tightness or a burning sensation in the area from the lower calf to the heel, particularly when rising from bed	Be sure to warm up thoroughly and stretch frequently, as shown on pages 35 and 67. Strengthen your calves, as shown on page 34. Take it easy when you run or walk uphill. If pain persists or is disabling, consult a physician.
Ankle sprain Acute pain, especially when standing or walking, and swelling of the ankle	Apply ice immediately after spraining, elevate the leg and use compression. Ice your ankle as often as possible for the first few days following your injury. If your ankle cannot bear weight, see a physician.
Black toenails A sometimes painful condition resulting from blood collecting underneath the toenails, which will fall off if left untreated	Have a physician puncture the toenail to release the blood and prevent loss of the toenail. To avoid recurrences, make sure your shoes have enough toe room.
Blisters Most common in the summer when perspiration increases friction between your feet and shoes, irritating skin	Clean the area around the blister carefully and puncture through the adjacent skin with a sterile needle to drain the fluid. If the blister becomes infected, remove the top of the blister completely. To avoid blisters, rub petroleum jelly over the balls of your feet, your heels and other blister-prone spots.
Chafing Redness and discomfort of the skin, usually on the inner thighs or nipples	Friction between the skin and clothing or between skin rubbing against skin causes this problem. Rub petroleum jelly on troublesome areas, or wear soft, nonbinding clothing. Nylon fabric may also help.
Cuboid bone displacement Pain or tenderness on the outside of the ankle that is difficult to pinpoint, resulting in an inability to push off the toes when running or walking	This is an acute injury that can occur suddenly, especially after running or walking over rugged terrain. If pain persists, see a podiatrist.
Delayed muscle soreness Muscle soreness and stiffness a day or two after exercise, such as a race or excessive downhill running	Warm up and stretch adequately before exercise. Running or walking will relieve the soreness, but be sure to exercise at a lower intensity.
Dizziness A feeling of faintness caused by a sudden drop in blood pressure, especially after standing up from a seated position	This is often a symptom of overtraining. Cut back slightly on your exercise program. If you feel dizzy while running or walking on a warm day, however, you may be dehydrated. Stop immediately and drink plenty of cool water. If dizziness persists, consult a physician.
Groin strain Pain or tightness on the inside of the thighs, resulting in a loss of stability and control as you swing your legs forward	Perform gentle stretches for the adductor muscles, such as the exercise shown on page 69. Warm up sufficiently before running or walking.

COMPLAINT/SYMPTOMS	PREVENTION AND RECOVERY TIPS
Hamstring pull Pain, tightness or swelling in the back of the thigh, forcing a shortened stride that is lacking in power	Be sure to warm up before exercising and take extra time to stretch your hamstrings and quadriceps. *See pages 35, 36 and 68.*
Heel spur Pain and swelling just under the heel bone, sometimes accompanied by pain and tenderness along the bottom of the foot	Stretch and strengthen the calf muscles, as shown on pages 34-35 and 67. Make sure your shoes have adequate arch support.
Iliotibial band pain Discomfort, tenderness or burning sensation on the outside of the knee, sometimes radiating up the side of the thigh	Reduce your mileage and workout intensity, and avoid hills and excessive running in one direction on graded roads. Make sure your shoes prevent excessive pronation of your feet.
Lower back pain Back muscle spasms or pain when bending or stretching your back	Strengthen your abdominal muscles, as shown on pages 120-123. Also, perform the lower back stretch, as shown on page 69.
Neuroma Numbness, tingling, pain or burning sensation between or under the toes	Make sure your shoes allow adequate toe room and have good forefoot cushioning. If pain persists, see a podiatrist.
Runner's knee Pain behind or around the kneecap	Avoid sprinting and excessive workouts on hills. Make sure your shoes prevent excessive pronation of your feet.
Sciatica Pain or cramping in the thighs and buttocks; tingling or numbness on the outside of the feet and toes	Avoid hill workouts. Be sure to perform hamstring and lower back stretches, as shown on pages 36 and 69. If pain persists, consult a physician.
Shin splints Discomfort, tenderness or burning pain along the shins	Warm up gradually, and run or walk on soft surfaces. If pain is acute, stop altogether for a few days. If pain persists, it may be due to a stress fracture; consult a physician.
Side stitch Muscle cramps, usually in the upper right abdomen, when running or walking	Stop and take deep breaths. Perform side stretches, as shown on pages 34 and 66. If you are in a race and do not wish to stop, make sure your posture is erect, and take deep abdominal breaths.
Stress fracture Dull ache accompanied by local tenderness and swelling; pain returns even after resting a few days	Persistent shin splints are often a sign of stress fractures. If you suspect a stress fracture, consult a physician.

Choosing Shoes

The most important piece of equipment you need for either walking or running is a good pair of shoes. Shoe manufacturers produce a wide selection of walking and running shoes, some of which are represented at right.

Shoes designed for runners, such as the pair shown on the bottom of the opposite page, generally have thick cushions. When selecting a running shoe, however, you must balance the benefits of good cushioning with the shoe's flexiblity — its ability to bend easily. Generally, the greater the cushioning and the thicker the sole, the less flexible the shoe is. Taller, heavier individuals should have shoes with greater cushioning; shorter, thinner people should find more flexible shoes.

Walking shoes, such as the pair shown at bottom right, require less cushioning than running shoes. When buying either walking or running shoes, look for heel counters or other stability features that control excessive pronation, or leaning inward toward the ankles. The shoes should also have leather or leather and mesh uppers, be flexible enough to bend easily at the ball of the foot, and have enough space for you to wiggle your toes.

If you plan to purchase shoes for hiking, orienteering or walking across rugged terrain, be sure they provide adequate ankle support, such as the pair at top left. If you engage in a variety of fitness activities and do not wish to purchase shoes for each application, look for cross-trainers, like those at top opposite, which combine characteristics of many types of shoes, including cushioning and heel support for walking and jogging, and ankle support and added stability for lifting weights and other activities.

Equipment

In addition to a good pair of shoes, walkers and runners can benefit from additional items such as those pictured at left. Many exercise walkers, for instance, enhance the benefits of walking by carrying hand weights such as those shown at bottom center. Many fitness enthusiasts and virtually all competitive walkers and runners wear digital wrist watches called chronographs. Besides displaying the time, a chronograph *(bottom center)* can function as a stopwatch for timing yourself.

Hikers who spend a whole day —or perhaps several days — on the trail must depend on a good backpack to carry supplies, and frame packs, such as the one shown opposite, take the weight off the shoulders and distribute it to the hips, buttocks and thighs. Day hikers, who may carry only a plastic water bottle and a sandwich or fruit, may prefer a fanny pack *(lower left)*, which is a belt with a pouch attached to the back so that it is light and snug.

If you hike in unfamiliar territory, you will also need a topographical map and a protractor compass similar to the examples shown here. Topographical maps clearly show geographical features, trails and elevations; the protractor compass, which has a housing that turns on a clear plastic rectangular base plate, allows you to align your map to magnetic north to find your way in the wilderness. *(See pages 54-59 for tips on how to use a map and compass.)*

CHAPTER TWO

Walking for Fitness

Techniques to make walking an effective aerobic conditioner

At first glance, walking may not seem like exercise; after all, virtually everybody does it. Many exercise physiologists, however, contend that it is an ideal activity for anyone who wants to get into shape. Walking is the safest and most convenient form of exercise for most people to engage in when they begin an exercise program. And since it is versatile — you can vary the intensity, the setting and the style of your workouts and you can race — walking is also appropriate as a long-term exercise, even for those who are already in good physical condition.

The greatest advantage to walking as a means to fitness is also, ironically, its biggest drawback — walking is efficient, which means it does not require much energy. Because of this, you can walk for long periods without taxing yourself. At a casual pace, in fact, walking is about twice as efficient as running: While a runner lifts himself off the ground, fighting gravity, a walker uses gravity to his advantage. With each walking stride, you fall forward from one foot, swinging the other leg ahead while gathering speed and energy. Then, when your forward leg strikes the ground and you begin to rise up on that leg, the energy is stored and then released when you stride forward, only to be gathered up and stored once again in the next gait cycle. The biomechanics of walking is similar to an egg rolling on end: You only have to add a tiny push with each roll to keep it moving. This finely tuned system of energy storage and retrieval means that a person walking at approximately 2.5 mph recovers 65 to 70 percent of the energy he expends with each stride.

Researchers have noted that walking efficiency decreases and the energy you expend increases as you quicken your pace. While a runner burns about the same number of calories to run a mile, regardless of the speed, the faster a walker covers a mile, the more calories he burns. The crossover point of efficiency between walking and running — that is, when the energy cost of walking exceeds that of running — is about five to 5.5 miles per hour. In one study, 10 well-conditioned men aged 22 to 39 were asked to walk at a fast pace for 30 minutes. Walking at about five miles an hour, all were able to achieve and maintain a pace intense enough to reach their target heart rate, proving that walking is actually an excellent form of exercise for young people who are very fit.

This chapter will show you how to make walking an effective exercise, whether you simply want to improve your overall cardiovascular conditioning, to lose weight or to derive aerobic benefits from outdoor leisure-time activity like orienteering or backpacking. There are several different ways to walk for fitness, as the following pages will show, and you can vary your walking workout to suit your mood or your training goals.

If you are beginning a walking program, you should start by walking briskly or striding at a pace that raises your heart rate to within 65 percent of your maximum for about 15 minutes *(see the chart on page 13)*. Warm up for five to 10 minutes before starting the walk, and cool down for an equal time afterward *(see pages 34-37 for warm-ups and cool-downs)*. Be sure to swing your arms vigorously. Walk on alternate days, gradually increasing your pace and distance until you can walk at a continuous, brisk pace for 20 to 60 minutes. Do not worry if you find it is uncomfortable to walk much faster. Many people can derive an aerobic benefit from walking at a pace of 3.5 to 4.5 mph.

You can increase the effort of walking in other ways besides increasing your speed. Carrying hand weights *(see page 43)* boosts the intensity yet allows you to maintain a comfortable pace. If you pump your arms while you carry hand weights, you will get a workout for your upper body as well as your lower body, and you will make your heart work harder. In addition to boosting the cardiovascular benefits of exercise walking, carrying weights while pumping your arms burns more calories than walking without weights. If you are just beginning a walking program, do not carry hand weights at first. You should be able to walk a 15-minute mile before you intensify your workout by carrying weights.

Climbing stairs is another excellent way to keep in shape and add to your lifelong fitness routine. If you live or work in a high-rise building, for example, you should make it a habit to walk up and down the stairs instead of riding the elevator. Studies of several groups of office employees showed that those who made use of the stairs instead of depending on the elevators improved their fitness levels by 10 to 15 percent.

You can also condition your body by augmenting weekday exercise walking with more strenuous weekend hikes. Hiking and backpacking are pleasant pastimes that help you maintain your aerobic conditioning and produce other health benefits. One Appalachian Trail hiker was tested by exercise physiologists before and after his 87-day, 1,700-mile trek, during which he carried a backpack weighing from 35 to 50 pounds. Because he was already in superb condition, his heart rate while hiking usually hovered somewhat below his target heart range, and his aerobic conditioning at the end of the hike was almost identical to his superb prehike level. But blood tests revealed that his HDL cholesterol, the "good" cholesterol that helps protect against arterial plaque, had risen from 54 to 74. This hiker's experience supports the research findings that frequent long-term activity — even if it is not within a formal workout setting or always intense enough to bring the heart to its target rate — can reduce the risk of cardiovascular disease.

You do not have to hike the Appalachian Trail to reap the benefits of backpacking: One study of 44 individuals aged 18 to 23 examined the effects of walking at a speed of 3.1 mph with a light backpack. It showed that walking for 30 minutes a day five days a week for three weeks with a load of six to 13 pounds significantly improved aerobic fitness levels. Although backpacking can be a strenuous activity, it is also reasonably safe: Fitness enthusiasts should carry loads of 35 pounds or less. Backpacking one or two days a week can add variety as well as vigor to any walking program. (*See page 53 for tips on hiking and backpacking.*)

Orienteering is another walking activity that is becoming popular in America. Since an orienteer's goal is to find a cross-country route between two points and then hike across terrain that may be quite rugged, this sport can be as challenging mentally as it is demanding physically. Those experienced in orienteering use a map and compass to help guide them along country roads and paths, and through the woods, fields and mountains. The ability to find your way through the wilderness is an admirable skill, and pathfinding can be an excellent addition to your regular fitness routine. By practicing a few simple techniques, you can learn orienteering easily and chart your own course. You can also take part in organized orienteering events. (*See page 54 for a more complete description of orienteering and a sample cross-country course.*)

If you enjoy the thrill of competing, or it helps you to feel motivated, you may want to try organized race walking. Race walking is the fastest form of walking: A typical race walker can walk as fast as many people can run. Indeed, the winner of the 20-kilometer walk at the 1988 Seoul Olympics averaged a speed of 9.3 mph for 12.4 miles for an Olympic record.

The race walker's special gait, however, is as different from ordinary walking as walking is from running. While a runner's feet leave the ground to extend his stride, a race walker's stride is increased by rotational, or rolling, movements of the hips. Early race walkers were called wobblies because of their style. Race walkers can achieve speeds that would be impossible for other walkers to attain. Since the crossover of efficiency between walking and running occurs between five and 5.5 mph, race walking at a faster speed burns more calories than running. Studies show that the body fat compositions and aerobic capacities of competitive race walkers are similar to those of marathon runners.

Race-walking technique is governed by a stringent set of rules designed to keep at least one of the race walker's feet in contact with the ground at all times. In other words, the heel of the lead foot must strike the ground before the toe of the back foot is lifted. This prevents "lifting," or rising up off the ground like a runner and gaining unfair advantage over other race walkers. You can race walk strictly for fitness, or you can train to enter races. Olympic athletes compete in long-distance walks of 20 kilometers (12.4 miles) and 50 kilometers (31 miles), but race walkers compete in walks of many shorter distances. Road-racing officials often allow separate entries for both race walkers and runners. By competing in running events, race walkers frequently derive impish pleasure from finishing ahead of many runners. Extremely popular in Mexico and Europe, race walking is now catching on in the United States. There are approximately 45,000 race walkers registered currently with the Walkers Club of America, including many competitors over the age of 40.

Walking of any kind can be a social activity to share with friends or family. You can converse while you walk, and you can combine walking with other activities such as sightseeing, visiting or doing errands. And if you like participating in organized activities, there are numerous walking events and groups to join. In the United States, there are an estimated 10,000 walking events annually, from walk-a-thons to competitive race walks that attract thousands of participants. And there are at least 6,500 walking clubs across the nation.

Many shopping malls encourage exercise walking, and even mark out walking courses, give away T-shirts and promote walking clubs and seminars in many areas. Malls and other indoor locations are particularly suited to walkers recovering from heart attacks or elderly persons who need to exercise, yet require a climate-controlled environment to provide protection against inclement weather, pollutants and allergy-provoking pollen.

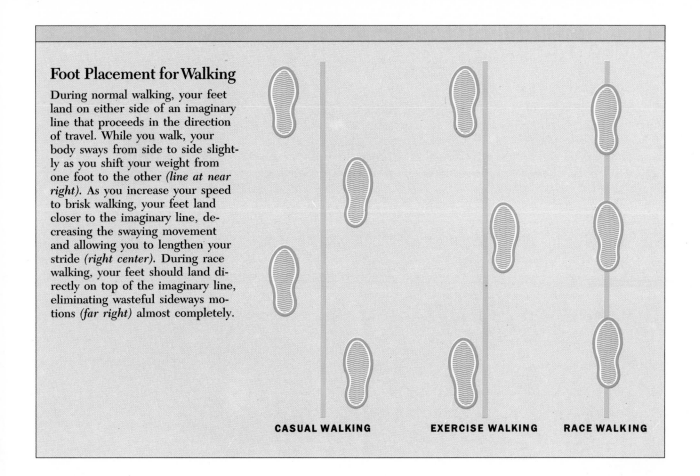

Foot Placement for Walking

During normal walking, your feet land on either side of an imaginary line that proceeds in the direction of travel. While you walk, your body sways from side to side slightly as you shift your weight from one foot to the other (*line at near right*). As you increase your speed to brisk walking, your feet land closer to the imaginary line, decreasing the swaying movement and allowing you to lengthen your stride (*right center*). During race walking, your feet should land directly on top of the imaginary line, eliminating wasteful sideways motions (*far right*) almost completely.

CASUAL WALKING   **EXERCISE WALKING**   **RACE WALKING**

Walking enthusiasts often insist that walking is safer than running and many other fitness activities because it is a low-impact sport that results in few injuries. It is true that the impact force of the foot against the ground is quite low in casual walking; however, that impact probably increases substantially during more energetic fitness walking. In addition, while a runner's knee is usually bent on foot strike, allowing the muscles to absorb much of the force of impact, the walker's knee remains straight, and may therefore transmit more of the shock of foot strike to the upper body. Fitness experts suspect that, because of their gait and the speed at which they travel, race walkers probably risk the same injuries as runners. (*For a description of the types of injuries you can sustain while walking, and how to avoid them, see pages 22-23.*)

The clothing you wear while you walk should be comfortable and nonrestrictive, such as loose-fitting street clothes or a warm-up suit. Race walkers usually wear the same outfits as runners. In winter, be sure to wear a wool cap and gloves to help you retain body heat, which is easily lost at the extremities. If you walk along paved roads, walk against the traffic and wear bright clothing during the day and reflective patches at night. (*For tips on finding the right walking shoes, see pages 24-25.*)

Warm-ups and Stretches/1

Each walking workout should be composed of three segments: warm-up, exercise and cool-down. A warm-up is the preliminary period or practice episode during which you begin to raise your heart rate and metabolic rate to the approximate level of the exercise session. In this way, your heart and muscles will be fully prepared to work for an extended period. Additionally, a warm-up prepares you mentally and helps you fine-tune your motor skills for your workout.

Warming up is important, and it is really quite simple to perform. All you have to do is rehearse your activity at a slightly lower intensity than normal. Make it a practice to warm up for five to 10 minutes.

You should also stretch, either after your warm-up or to cool down at the end of your exercise session. Stretching will increase the range of motion in your joints and develop greater muscle flexibility. The stretching routine shown on these two pages and the following two was designed specifically for walkers. Perform each stretch for at least 20 seconds. Be sure to repeat a stretch for one side of your body on the other side as well.

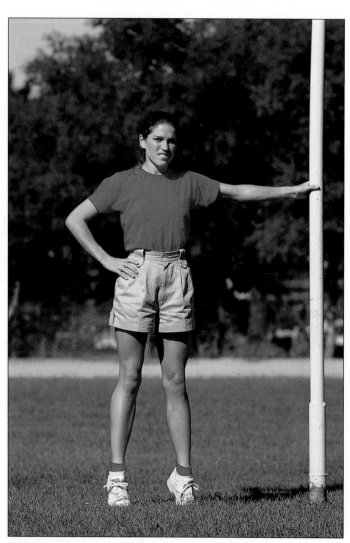

Perform heel raises to stretch and strengthen your calf muscles. Hold on to a stationary object for balance and stand on your toes. Then drop your heels to the ground. Perform at least 20 heel raises.

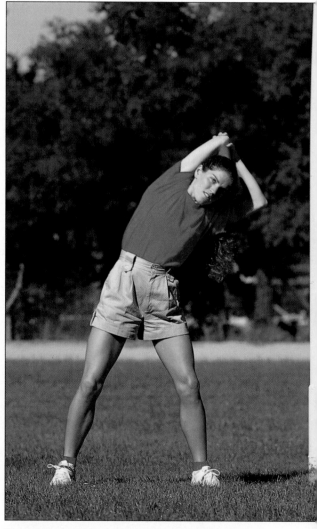

To stretch your side muscles, grasp your right elbow with your left hand over your head. With your feet apart and knees bent slightly, pull your elbow to the left until you feel a stretch.

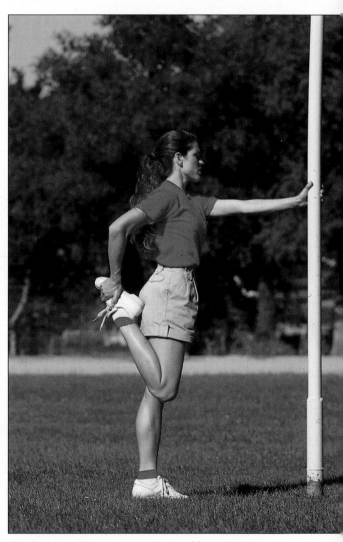

Hold on to a stationary object with both hands. Extend your right leg behind you and bend your left knee. Lean forward until you feel a stretch in your calf and Achilles tendon.

Stabilize yourself against a stationary object with your left hand. Bend your right knee and grasp your right foot with your right hand. Pull your knee toward your buttocks until you feel a stretch in your thigh.

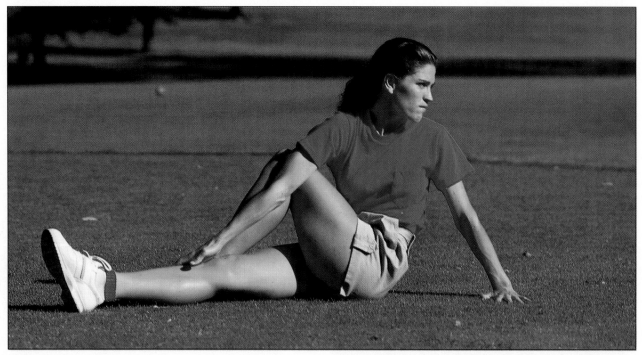

Sit on the ground and support yourself with your left arm *(above)*. Extend your right leg and place your left foot outside your right knee. Place your right elbow against your left knee and twist to the left.

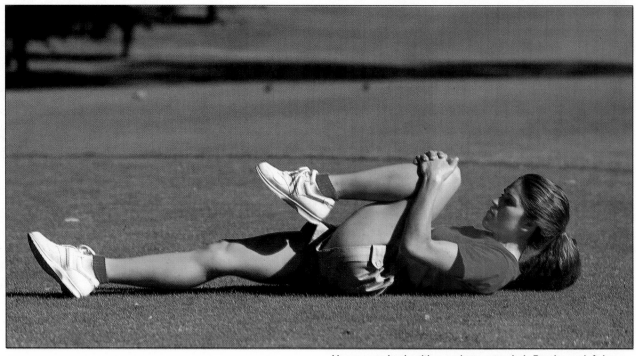

Lie on your back with your legs extended. Bend your left knee and grasp it with both hands. Lift your head and draw your knee toward your chest until you feel a stretch in your thigh and buttock *(above)*.

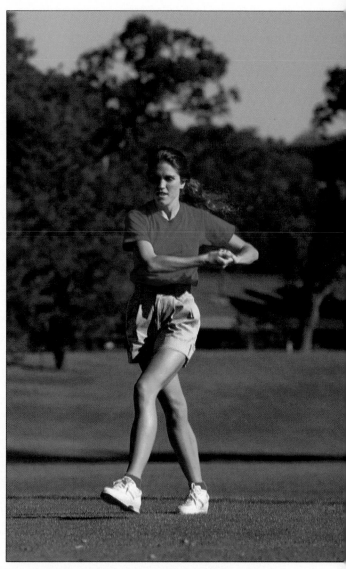

Perform windmills to improve flexibility in your shoulders. Walk at a brisk pace and swing your arms in full circles, alternating sides as if you were performing the backstroke in the water.

To increase hip mobility, cup your hands together and swing them from side to side as you walk briskly. Use a crossover stride so that your left foot is placed on the outside line of your right foot, and vice versa.

Walking Stride/1

Normal walking is biomechanically efficient — that is, it does not require much energy. However, as your walking speed increases, your efficiency decreases. The faster you walk, therefore, the faster your heart beats and the more calories you burn. By the time you are walking at a pace of five miles per hour, you are burning about the same number of calories as if you were running. At higher speeds than this, it is easier and more efficient to run than to walk.

The key to walking efficiently at slow speeds is the biomechanics of the walking gait. As the photographs on these and the following pages show, the proper posture and stride will make your technique efficient.

While walking, you always keep at least one foot in contact with the ground. The foot on the ground supports the body while the raised foot swings forward. In addition, there is a brief period when both feet are in contact with the ground. At slow speeds, this gait conserves energy. At speeds above 3.5 miles per hour, however, it takes an increasing amount of energy to keep both feet on the ground. Therefore, to burn more calories and improve your fitness, you should walk as fast as you can comfortably.

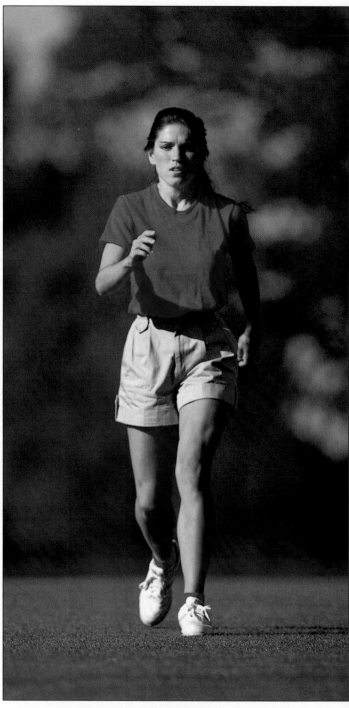

Push off with your right foot and shift your weight to your left leg. During the left-leg support phase, your right leg is free to swing forward.

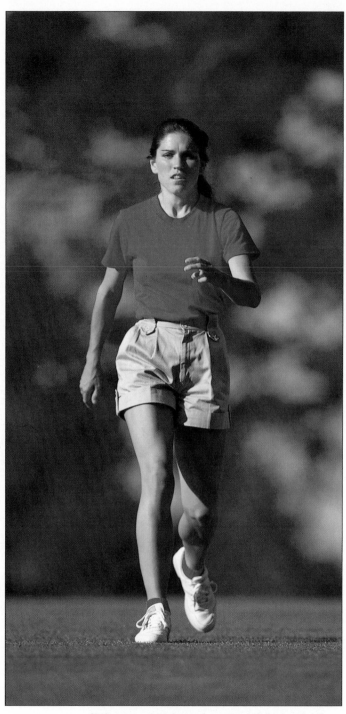

At the completion of the right-leg swing phase, strike the ground with your right heel and roll forward on your left foot. There is a moment of double support.

Shift your weight forward on your left foot and roll forward from the right heel. By the time you push off from your toes, your right leg supports your body.

Walking Stride/2

To get the most from walking, swing your arms forcefully with each stride. At your right heel strike *(1)*, raise your left hand to about chin level. As you begin to shift your weight onto your right foot during the double-support phase *(2)*, swing your left arm down for balance. Both arms are close to your sides *(3)* during midstance. As you shift your weight forward from your right foot *(4)*, swing your right arm up to balance your left leg. Then, just before your left heel strike *(5)*, raise your right hand toward chin level.

Increasing the Effort

Virtually anyone can improve his or her fitness by walking regularly. However, a person who is already well conditioned may have to walk uncomfortably fast in order to raise his heart rate to its training zone. For an explanation of the training zone and how you can determine yours, see page 17. For instance, one study showed that fit young men may have to walk at a pace of five miles per hour or more to achieve their training heart rates.

Fortunately, walking at high speed is not the only way to get a quality walking workout even if you are very fit. Studies show that you can increase your workload significantly by carrying hand weights of one to three pounds, so long as you swing your arms vigorously and maintain a brisk pace.

You can also increase the intensity by choosing hilly terrain as your walking course. It takes more than twice as much energy, for instance, to walk briskly up a moderate incline than it would simply to walk briskly along a flat stretch.

While carrying hand weights, be sure to swing them vigorously. When walking up hills, shorten your stride slightly. Do not slacken your pace but keep your head up while you lean into the hill.

Common Walking Mistakes

I t is important to maintain good form and posture while you walk. Keeping your head up, your pelvis back and your abdomen tight will improve your respiration and blood circulation.

Yet, because walking is such an automatic activity, many people exhibit poor posture while walking. Poor posture makes you unbalanced and forces the muscles in your head and body to strain to keep your balance. In addition to increasing fatigue, poor walking habits may result in lower back pain, shin splints and neck and shoulder aches.

These two pages show some common indicators of faulty posture. Monitor yourself from time to time to make sure you are not straining or tightening up, which may indicate fatigue or bad posture.

Slumping can cause neck and lower back pain *(right)*. Tighten your stomach, pull in your buttocks and swing your arms.

Neck and lower back pain can also result from watching your feet *(above)*. Keep your back erect and head up.

If your hands and teeth are clenched, then you are probably tense and stiff *(above)*. Concentrate on relaxing.

Target Heart Rate Zone

Do not walk with ankle weights *(below left)*, which may throw off your leg momentum. Avoid bending your elbows when using hand weights *(center)*; you might hit your head. Do not hold hand weights at your sides limply *(right)*, since that will not improve walking intensity.

Swinging your arms to the sides indicates you are throwing energy away from your direction of travel *(right)*.

Take smooth, even strides, but do not try to overreach your step, which can strain your muscles *(left)*.

Race Walking/1

You can walk faster, and thus burn more calories in a shorter period of time, by race walking than by walking in any other style. The race walker minimizes the double-support phase to a fraction of a second and employs a rolling hip movement to extend the stride length and frequency.

Competitive race walking is governed by two basic rules to prevent "lifting," or rising off the ground with both feet. First, the advancing foot must make contact with the ground before the rear foot leaves the ground; and second, the supporting leg must be straight in the vertically upright position.

Start race walking slowly, so you can become accustomed to the gait.

Point your toes in the direction of your stride and swing your right leg forward, reaching with your hip and knee so that you strike the ground with your heel at about a 40-degree angle. Be sure that your leg is straight when your heel hits the ground. Push off with your left foot and keep your right leg straight as your body passes over it to begin the gait cycle again.

Arm movements are also important in race walking: They add thrust to each stride and assist in giving you balance and momentum. Although race walking may feel like an unnatural movement at first, with practice you should soon feel as if you were gliding lightly or even floating smoothly across the ground.

Keep your leg straight when your right heel strikes the ground *(1)*. Be sure your leg remains straight as your body assumes a vertically upright position *(2)*. Roll forward on your right foot and swing your left leg in front of you *(3)*. Push off with the toes of your right foot and extend your left leg *(4)*, making sure that it is straight at heel strike *(5)*. Swing your right leg forward *(6)* and roll toward your toes on your left foot *(7)*. Finally, push off on your toes and straighten your right leg for heel strike *(8)*.

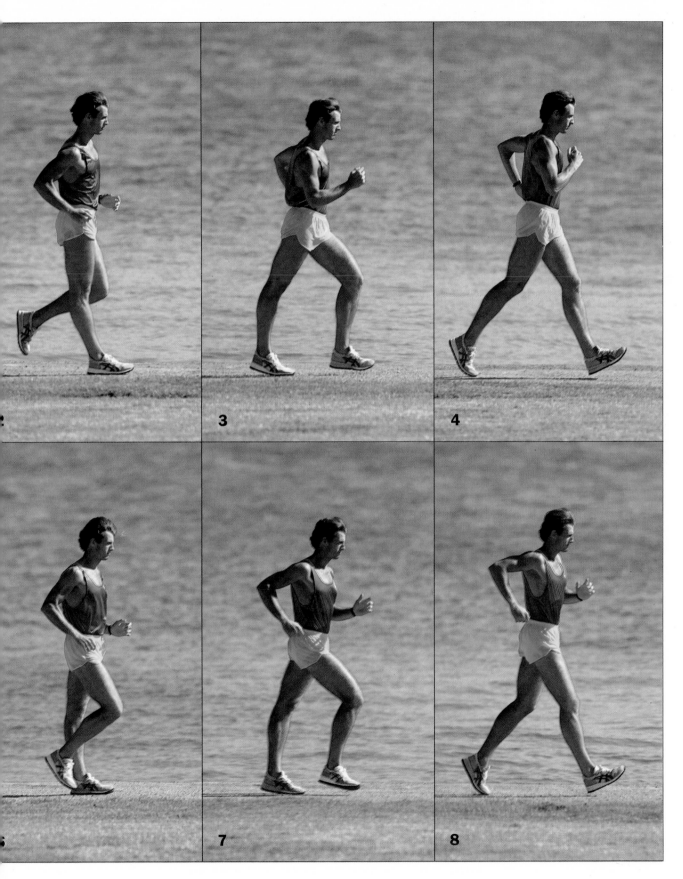

Race Walking/2

While race walking, one heel must strike the ground before the toes of your other foot lose contact. Plant your feet in a heel-to-toe alignment so that you will be walking along an imaginary line *(left)*.

Bend your arms at a 90-degree angle, and keep your hands turned in and cupped slightly. Swing them from just behind your hips to mid-chest level *(1)*. During midstance, your hands should be in front of your hips *(2)*. As you swing your right leg forward, move your left hand forward for balance *(3)*. Return to midstance with the right leg supporting your body *(4)*.

Common Race-Walking Mistakes

In the beginning, you will have to pay particular attention to your walking form. And even after you have mastered race walking, and your technique has become second nature, you should review your form periodically to make sure you have not picked up any bad habits. Even top-ranked race walkers develop sloppy form, especially when they are fatigued.

Do not look down at your feet or watch your hands to see if you are race walking correctly. Instead, try to stay relaxed and loose. If you feel tension in your body, it may be caused by a mistake that is detracting from your performance. It is often a good idea to train with a partner, who can easily spot errors in your form that you do not notice.

Pictured on this page are the results of three common race-walking mistakes; on the facing page are three errors in technique that judges look for and can lead to your disqualification from a race-walking event or competition.

Walk erect with your buttocks in and your stomach muscles tight *(above)*. **Excessive curvature of the spine can result in lower back pain.**

Do not swing your arms across your chest, since it will cause excessive rotational movements of your shoulders and upper body *(left)*.

This results in a swaying, side-to-side motion and shortens the distance of each stride *(above)*. **Plant your feet along an imaginary straight line.**

Technical Errors

LIFTING Keep your rear foot on the ground until the heel of your leading foot makes contact *(left)*.

HANDS TOO HIGH Carrying your arms high and close to your chest raises your center of gravity and may mean you are lifting off the ground *(right)*.

BENT-KNEE FOOT STRIKE Make sure your knee is straight when your leading foot hits the ground *(left)*. A bent knee can lead to disqualification in a race-walking event.

Hiking

In the past 15 years or more, increasing numbers of Americans have participated in fitness routines such as walking and running and in wilderness pursuits such as camping and canoeing. Hiking combines the elements of both, providing a challenging workout for anyone who loves the outdoors. Although it is not possible for most people to take hikes daily, many exercise walkers find that weekend hikes and backpacking trips provide another dimension to their usual fitness workouts.

In addition to its value as a break in a walker's routine and as an adventure in itself, hiking can be a powerful aerobic conditioner. Although few studies have quantified the benefits of hiking, the experience of hikers themselves makes clear that hiking is a strenuous activity that demands a high degree of fitness. One group of hikers and researchers from the Georgia Institute of Technology, for instance, determined that hiking 150 miles in 13 days is the rough equivalent of running five miles in 40 minutes or less.

Orienteering/1

In addition to its practical value as a means to get around in the wilderness, orienteering — using a map and compass to find your path between points of land — has special sports and fitness applications. Orienteering clubs across the nation regularly hold meets, in which entrants are given special topographic-style maps indicating a series of checkpoints, called controls, to find. Hikers must proceed from one control to the next to complete a course. (For tips on selecting the right type of compass, see page 27.)

On most orienteering maps, the start of a course is drawn as a triangle, the finish as two concentric circles and controls as single circles. Control markers, usually white and red or orange flags, are placed on the course. Some control markers may be easy to find, while others may be placed behind a landmark. Lines connecting the control markers show the shortest routes between them, but not necessarily the most desirable ones. These two pages and the following four show a sample orienteering progression from an easily located control marker in the middle of a field to a control marker placed behind a tree.

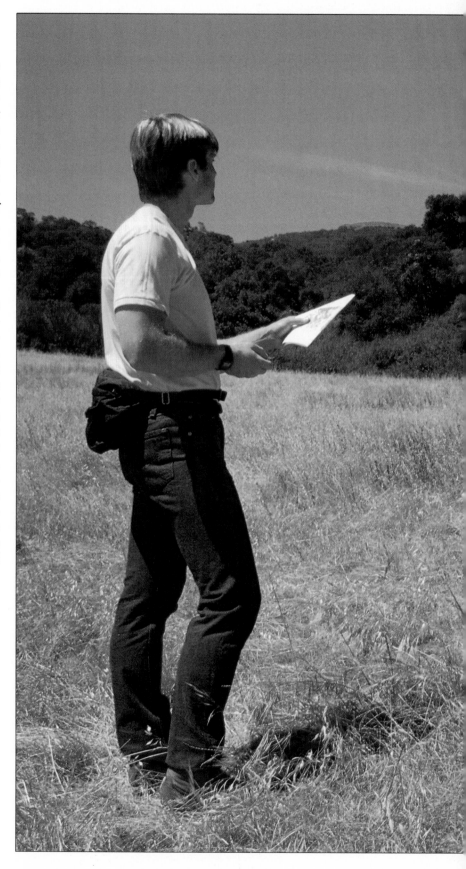

Stand near the control marker and relate your map to the landscape *(right)*. **On the map** *(opposite, top)*, **you are standing at the first control after the triangle in the middle of an open area. The top of the map is north, and you can see the line of trees and heavy vegetation (shown as green patches) to the north and east. Although the most direct route is through the vegetation, a more practical route may be to head north until you hit a trail (line of dashes), where you turn right. Then you can walk southeast to the top of a hill (thin brown contour lines). From there — the attack point — you can plot your route to the second control, which is a tree (small green circle in the center of the control circle). Having chosen your route, strike out in a northern direction** *(opposite, bottom)* **until you hit the trail.**

Orienteering/2

Once you have made it to the top of the hill, you have reached your attack point. If you cannot see the control, then kneel down and place the map on your thigh *(left)*. Place your compass on top of the map and orient the map so that the red compass needle points to the north end. Then position the base plate of the compass on the map so that one edge connects both where you are now, at the top of the hill, and your destination, the next control. Turn the housing of the compass so that the red needle points to both north on the map and north on the housing *(above)*. Since north on orienteering maps is actually magnetic north, to find the next control, merely follow the compass heading — in this case, 120 degrees— shown by the arrow on the compass base.

Orienteering/3

After you have set your bearing, stand up and hold the compass in front of you, with the arrow on the base plate pointing straight ahead *(above)*. Keeping the red compass arrow pointing north, walk in a straight line. If you continue walking in the direction you have plotted, you should soon see the tree indicated on the map. The control marker will be behind it *(right)*.

CHAPTER THREE

Running
*For fun, for fitness and
for competition*

Running is a vigorous conditioner for most of the body's largest and most powerful muscles, especially the heart. Studies have shown repeatedly that running significantly improves cardiovascular fitness for almost everyone, including children and older people. One study has shown that people who began running programs lowered their blood pressure. And among athletes, the average VO_2max of elite distance runners, according to one survey, is higher than that of every other group of endurance athletes, including competitive cyclists and rowers, elite swimmers and world-class cross-country skiers. Runners in the same survey also showed a lower percentage of overall body fat than any other group.

Running also seems to have a beneficial effect on a person's state of mind: Runners commonly report that if they are anxious, angry or depressed, they feel better after a run, and psychological tests confirm that running tends to reduce feelings of stress and anxiety.

Running is justly promoted by many physicians and sports-medicine practitioners as both a preventative and therapeutic activity. No wonder that the President's Council on Physical Fitness and Sports determined that running, when compared to 13 other popular forms of exercise, was the best activity for cardiovascular fitness, muscle growth, losing weight and relaxation.

In addition to its direct physiological and psychological benefits, running seems to encourage people to eliminate bad habits and adopt a healthier lifestyle. Researchers in Georgia surveyed 1,250 randomly selected male and female entrants in the Peachtree Road Race in Atlanta. The researchers found that 81 percent of the men and 75 percent of the women who smoked cigarettes when they began recreational running had given up the habit by the time they entered this 6.2-mile (10-kilometer) race. They also determined that weight loss was associated with running: On the average, men who were overweight when they started running lost more than two pounds for every six miles they ran per week.

The key to many of these physiological benefits is the biomechanical action of the running stride. Although the gait is similar for both running and walking, there are significant differences between them. Speed is determined largely by how fast you can move your legs — your stride rate, style and gait technique — and how far each step reaches — your stride length. When you walk, you always have at least one foot on the ground, and there is a brief period of double support, during which both feet are on the ground. Although this makes the walking stride efficient, it slows you down. In contrast, when you run, you literally take off into the air with each stride. The period when you are in the air, called the float phase, accounts for about 30 percent of your stride. (*See the illustration on pages 70-71.*)

The great value of running as an aerobic conditioner derives in part from the effort required by three groups of the body's most powerful muscles to become airborne: the calves, hamstrings and the buttocks. In addition, the quadriceps muscle along the front of your thigh is required to pull your knee forward and draw it up to prepare your leg for its next stride cycle. Electromyographic measurements of the electrical activity in the leg muscles show that as you progress from walking to sprinting, your leg muscles become activated for longer periods of time. The hamstrings, for instance, are active during 10 percent of a walker's stance phase — when the foot is supporting the body — while the same tests show that the hamstrings are involved during 80 percent of a runner's stance phase. Similarly, the calf muscles work during 15 percent of a walker's stance phase compared to 80 percent of the runner's stance.

Some of the very factors that make running such a vigorous conditioner can also cause injuries. For instance, the ground reaction force, which is generated between your foot and the ground, either during push-off or upon impact, can amount to forces of up to 2.8 times your body weight during fast running and perhaps as high as 5.5 times

C an running replace psychotherapy? Researchers at San Diego State University gave 12 men and women, aged 23 to 41, a series of initial psychological evaluations. After a one-year program of running three times a week for 45 minutes, the people were retested. The researchers found that in addition to cardiovascular improvement, the subjects were found to be more relaxed, assertive, happy-go-lucky and able to deal with abstract concepts more effectively.

Problems with Heat and Cold

During hard exercise, muscles can produce 15 to 20 times the amount of heat that they produce at rest. This heat production can raise your body temperature rapidly. Your body can cool itself through the evaporation of sweat. But on hot, humid days or when you are dehydrated and you cannot produce enough sweat, you may not be able to dissipate the heat, causing hyperthermia, a dangerous build-up of internal heat. The early symptoms of this form of heat stress can include headache, nausea, dizziness, clumsiness and excessive sweating or no sweating at all.

Running at a comfortable pace, drinking plenty of fluids and wearing the proper clothing will go a long way toward helping you avoid hyperthermia. On warm days, you should also run in white or brightly colored clothing made out of cotton or another natural fiber that both reflects the radiant heat of sunlight and allows your body to cool itself through sweating.

Make sure you drink enough fluid before and after you run, or, if you are covering a long distance, during the run. Drink even if you are not thirsty, since you can lose two to three quarts of fluid before you notice a thirst and become dehydrated, which increases the likelihood of developing hyperthermia.

Plain water is the best liquid to drink. Have at least one eight-ounce glass before you begin your run, and at least another eight ounces after you have finished.

Do not run at all if the temperature approaches 90 degrees and the humidity exceeds 75 percent. Also, skip your run if it is hot and you feel a cold coming on.

Too much heat loss from the body, called hypothermia, is not as dangerous to runners as hyperthermia, but it can also present problems. Hypothermia can occur even on moderately cool days, especially in high altitudes or if it is damp and windy.

Early warning signs of hypothermia include shivering, a sense of elation and a feeling of intoxication. On cool and cold days, wear a polypropylene garment near the skin that "wicks" away moisture. Then wear several thin layers of cotton fabric for insulation, with a removable nylon windbreaker as an outer layer.

body weight during sprinting. Foot-strike impact can amount to a force of 30 Gs. This force causes a vibration that travels up your legs at 200 miles an hour like a shock wave to the top of your head.

The human body, however, is able to make a number of biomechanical adjustments to accommodate the effects of this shock wave. When you run, your body increases the flexion of the hips, knees and ankles, thereby lowering its center of gravity. At heel strike, the runner's flexed knee and ankle allow the contracted muscles that stabilize each joint to act as shock absorbers, which dissipate much of the force of impact. By the time that shock wave hits your hips, the impact has been dissipated to about one-sixth its original strength; when it reaches your head, it is less than one-tenth.

Despite the body's shock-absorbing capabilities, most runners are well aware that they are not immune to injury. In a survey of entrants to a 10-kilometer road race in New York City, researchers found that 46.6 percent of the respondents had sustained a running injury within the previous two years. Predictably, the researchers found that the injury rate increased with the number of miles run per week, the pace and the frequency of competitions entered. The injury rate, surprisingly, was not related to running surfaces, terrain or interval training, which entails spurts of fast running.

Fortunately, the recovery rate among runners was high: 76 percent of those who consulted a doctor reported a good or excellent recovery from their injuries. Moreover, most running injuries can be prevented, first and foremost by wearing a good pair of running shoes and by not pushing yourself too hard. *(For a review of running injuries and how to recover from them, see pages 22-23.)*

If you have never run before, or if you are out of shape, begin your training program by alternating brisk walking with slow jogging for 20 minutes three times a week. As your muscles and tendons become adjusted to the stress, gradually lengthen the time you run and shorten the walking time until you can sustain a run for the full 20 minutes. The guidelines and sample workouts on pages 20-21 show how to develop a program that is both varied and progressive.

Be sure to warm up properly before each workout and to cool down afterward. As you build up your stamina, you can pay more attention to your running form, which will increase your efficiency by reducing bouncing motions. The techniques shown on pages 70-77 will make running more enjoyable and also help you to avoid injury.

Ideally, running should be viewed not as a monotonous chore, but as a vacation, a retreat from life's daily demands. But while many people are perfectly happy performing a 20-minute meditative jog several times a week, others do become bored. If you are interested in adding variety and adventure to your running regimen, this chapter will show you some options you can pursue, from training with a partner to entering "fun runs" — races in which winning is not a concern — and various competitive events.

Studies show that runners who enter races and fun runs tend to become long-term fitness enthusiasts. The survey of Peachtree Road Race entrants determined that most of them appeared to be dedicated runners: Almost 90 percent of the men and 80 percent of the women were still running one year after the race. In addition to the motivation spur that competition provided for these runners, friends also worked as a support group, providing camaraderie.

Although you do not have to compete to be a good runner or to continue on a running program successfully, many people find that weekend races and fun runs provide motivation on many levels. Beginning runners, for instance, may be inspired to train well enough to complete a local three- or six-mile race. Objectives for more experienced runners may be to improve their time, complete a longer race or perhaps to finish before a friend or another runner who had been faster in a previous race.

Once you have entered some races, you may decide to train to improve your time. To be reasonably sure of completing a race, your minimum weekly mileage should be at least twice the distance of the race you plan to run. A weekly mileage base of 20 or more miles will

Pace and Posture

Runners experience slight but significant posture differences as they increase speed, as shown by the two figures at right, which are silhouettes of an elite middle-distance runner filmed while running on a treadmill. At six miles per hour — the equivalent of a 10-minute-mile jogging pace — the runner is more upright, his body has an up-and-down motion and his stride rate is moderate. When he doubles his speed to 12 miles per hour — the pace of an elite marathon runner — his body slants forward and his stride length and rate increase.

As you increase your running speed, therefore, you use new muscles or the same ones in slightly different ways. Exercise physiologists believe that to prepare for competition, you must train at about the same pace at which you plan to race, replicating race conditions as closely as possible. In this way, your muscles can rehearse the movements and postures they will undergo during the competition.

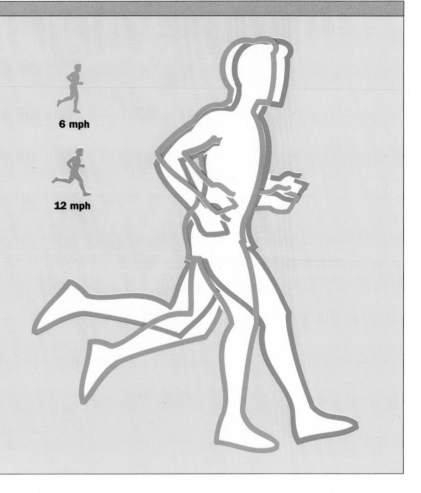

6 mph

12 mph

not only prepare you to finish the race, but will probably help you run stronger and faster.

In addition to accumulating miles to improve your endurance, your strength and speed will also be dramatically enhanced by running hills repeatedly, including running timed interval workouts on the track, and performing a technique called "fartlek," or "speed play." Developed by the coach of the 1948 Swedish Olympic Team, fartlek workouts are usually run with at least one other person and often consist of alternating easy running with untimed sprints over varied terrain. While on a fartlek run, you can play games such as tag, toss a ball back and forth or challenge your partner to short races. Since it helps boost performance, fartlek training is used by many runners.

By making up games to play while you run, by giving yourself attainable goals and by entering fun runs and weekend races, you can make running an enjoyable activity rather than just a solitary ordeal. Instead of giving you a rigid exercise prescription, this chapter will also give you some tips on entering races, which can be social events as well as self-motivating competitions.

Spread your feet and place your hands on your hips. Keeping your back straight, bend to the right, then forward, to the left and backward.

Stretches/1

Runners frequently rush through their preliminary stretches, or do not stretch at all. But stretching after warming up sufficiently is vital to your physical training because it increases joint range of motion and muscle suppleness, and thus helps prevent injury.

Flexibility will help you avoid injury in three ways: First, supple muscles and tendons are less prone to tears and strains than stiff muscles; second, flexible muscles and good joint range of motion reduce the chance of sprains; and third, muscle elasticity places less strain on adjacent joints. A runner with tight hamstrings, for instance, is not only at a higher risk for leg muscle and tendon injuries, he may also injure his knees, lower back and hips.

Be sure to warm up your muscles before you stretch. You can stretch before or after a run, as long as you warm up by running in place or taking a short jog first. Warming up increases the blood flow to the muscles and helps make them loose.

Do not bounce when you stretch; this "ballistic" stretching may actually injure the muscles you are trying to protect. Instead, always perform relaxed and deliberate stretches. Never push yourself to the point of pain, although the final stage of a stretch should be slightly uncomfortable.

Hold each of these stretches for 20 seconds and relax. You may repeat the stretch if you wish. If you perform a stretch on one side of your body, be sure to repeat the stretch on the opposite side.

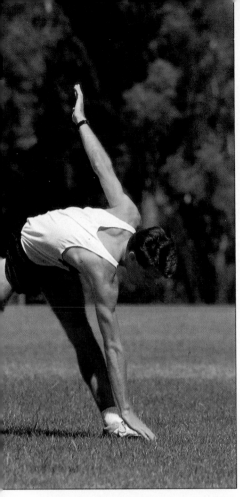

Hold your arms out to the sides, parallel to the ground with your feet spread, then bend at the waist and reach your right hand toward your left toes.

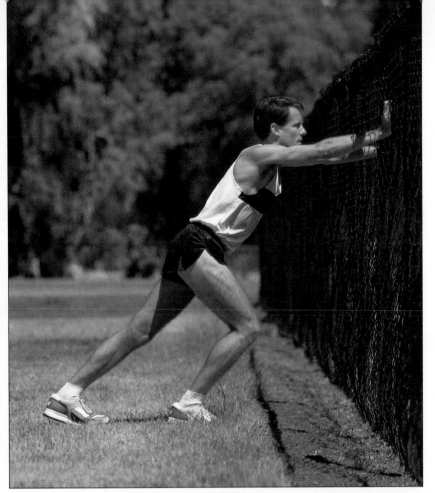

Place your hands against a fence. Bend your right knee and extend your left leg, easing your heel toward the ground until you feel a stretch in your calf (above).

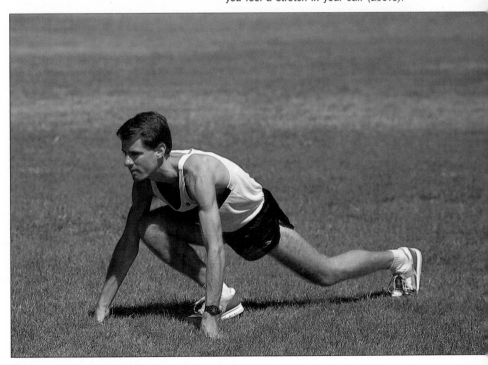

Squat on the ground, supporting yourself with your hands. Extend your left leg, drawing your right leg to your chest.

Lie on your back, bend your left knee, grasp it with both hands and draw it toward your chest *(top)*. Then extend your arms to the sides to stabilize your upper body, and cross your left leg over your right. Keeping both shoulders on the ground, extend your left foot toward your right hand *(above)*.

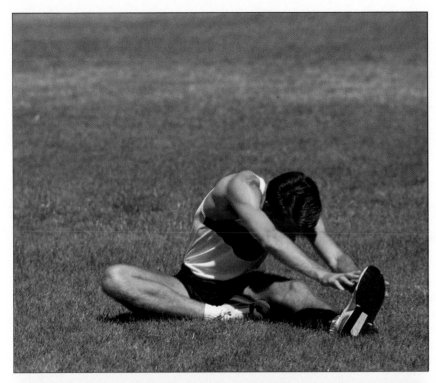

Sit on the ground, extend your left leg and draw your right foot to your left thigh. With both hands, slowly reach toward your extended foot *(left)*.

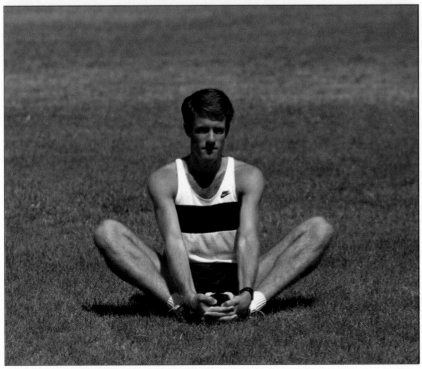

Sit on the ground and draw the soles of both feet together. Hold your feet and move your knees toward the ground as far as you can to stretch your adductor muscles *(left)*.

Running
Stride/1

Many runners mistakenly think of running as a bouncing motion rather than as a continuous movement, and you may notice that the heads of inexperienced runners often bounce. In fact, one researcher has calculated that an inexperienced marathoner may bounce so much that he runs the equivalent of a mile vertically.

In a truly efficient stride, such as the one shown here and on the following two pages, the runner's head barely moves up and down during any portion of the stride.

When you run, try to think of propelling yourself forward. If you do not bounce, your body will have a lower center of gravity, thus giving you a longer and more powerful drive. In addition, your knees and ankles will be more flexed, helping them to absorb road shock.

You can also use your arms to improve your running technique. Do not hold them limply at your sides when you run; pump them as if you were punching to improve your speed and power. The faster your arms move, the faster your legs move. Never let your hands swing away from your hips or across the middle of your chest. Allow your elbows to stick out slightly to counterbalance the rotation your feet make with each stride.

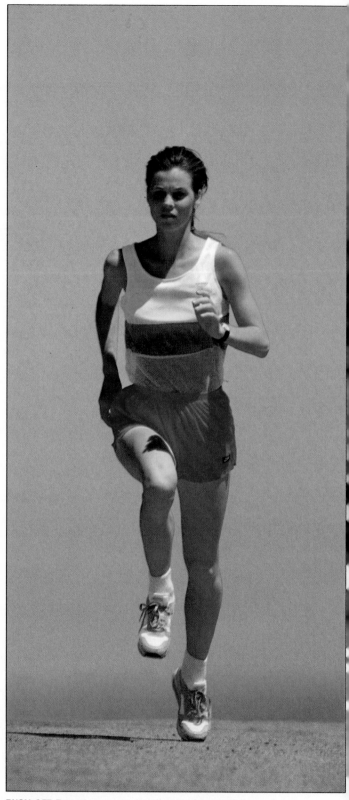

PUSH-OFF Extend your rear leg to propel yourself forward, not upward. Meanwhile, lift your front knee so that it pulls forward while the rear knee is extended. The calf muscles of your rear leg draw you up on your toes to push you forward.

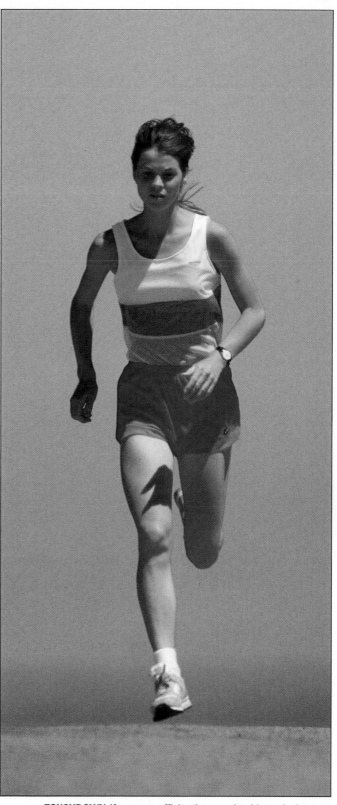

FLOAT After the push-off phase, your body becomes airborne. The float phase extends your stride so that you can move faster when you run than when you walk. Look ahead; looking down will shorten your stride.

TOUCHDOWN If you run efficiently, you should touch down on the outside rear of your foot, rather than on the heel, which allows greater weight distribution. You should feel more of a quick slap than a hard impact on the ground.

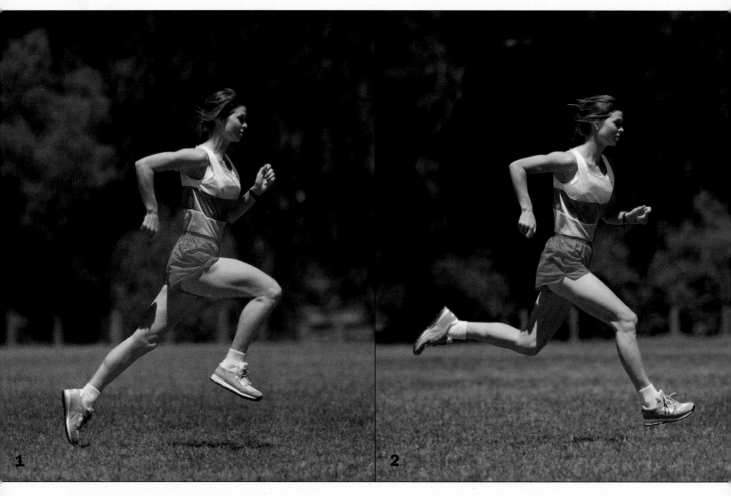

1

2

Running Stride/2

To maintain a relaxed stride, keep your shoulders back, chest out and buttocks in (1). During the float phase, do not over-extend your stride; allow your legs to extend naturally (2). As your hands swing back and forth, they should occasionally brush lightly against your shorts (3). If you feel tension in your shoulders, hands or jaw, remind yourself to relax; unclench your jaw, loosen your hands and drop your shoulders (4).

4

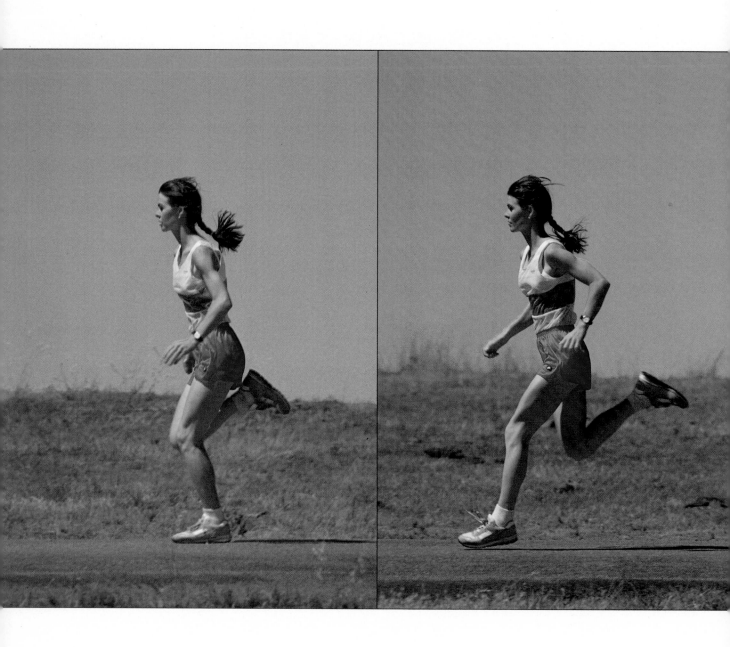

Sprinting

For fun, variety or during competition, you may want to increase your speed. Maintaining good form, though, becomes all the more important when you sprint. Since sprinting is essentially an anaerobic activity that requires more strength than endurance, you can become fatigued quickly. When this occurs, you rapidly lose your form, efficiency and speed.

The key to fast running is to train often and pay attention to your form. Do not worry about your pace at first. Just run as fast as you can for short distances — a block, for instance — without sacrificing your form. Once you become accustomed to running fast in good form, perform timed intervals on a track to increase your stamina and overall sprinting speed (*see pages 92-93*).

When sprinting, think of your feet as spokes of a wheel and keep them moving quickly. Use your arms to punch the air *(below)*. Your hands should never become fists or flop about; keep them relaxed and turn your palms in slightly *(below left)*. Maintain an erect posture and move forward on your feet so that you touch down close to your toes *(opposite right)*. Do not bounce, but slap the ground with your foot *(opposite left)*.

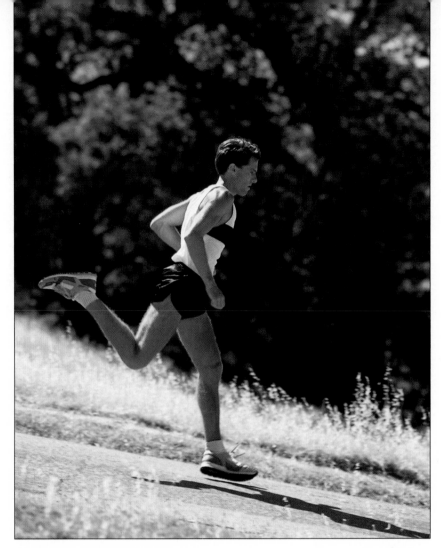

Learn to "fall" uphill by leaning forward; use a short stride and push from your toes. Pretend you are using your arms to pull yourself up a rope *(opposite)*. Do not sprint down a hill; stay relaxed and allow yourself to "fall" so that you can catch your breath, yet still maintain speed. Lean forward and land on the balls of your feet. Instead of pumping your arms, keep them low to maintain balance *(left)*.

Hills

Running uphill is taxing. However, nothing can help you build leg power better or condition you faster than hill work. In addition, it sharpens your mental toughness and builds the physical stamina required to race.

The technique of running uphill is fairly simple, although problems you have running on a flat surface are magnified once you go up a slope. Practice your technique by running hard up a quarter- to half-mile hill with a 10-15 percent grade. Do not stop at the crest; continue to run hard over the top. Then keep running downhill quickly but relaxed to regain your breath. Once you are on level ground, turn around to climb the hill again. Training in this manner is called running repeat hills. You may run repeat hills once or twice a week, but never on consecutive days, so that your body has a chance to recover.

Although running down a hill takes about two-thirds the amount of energy as running up the same hill, downhill runs are more jarring to your body and are more likely to cause injury. Also, downhill runs are more likely to leave you with sore muscles a day or two later, because your muscles will be unaccustomed to resisting the forward momentum. This soreness will diminish with continued training, however, as your muscles become more relaxed when running downhill. If possible, train on grass at first; you can become accustomed to the slope while keeping the impact to a minimum.

Common Running Mistakes

Running technique can be idiosyncratic and still be effective. And you would never be disqualified from a race for bad running form. However, many runners — especially beginners — make wasteful movements that detract from their performance and contribute to fatigue and injury.

If you watch a top-ranked long-distance runner during a marathon, you may think that he is running at a relaxed and leisurely pace. However, if you clock his pace, you may find that the leading contenders are run-ning five-minute miles. The key to this seemingly effortless movement is running efficiency: There is not a single wasted movement, and no sign of strain. Running five-minute miles for more than 26 miles is certainly not a leisurely pace; it only appears so because most elite runners maintain their form effectively.

You can improve your pace by eliminating wasteful movements that can drain your energy. These two pages illustrate the six most common mistakes that people make and suggest ways to correct them.

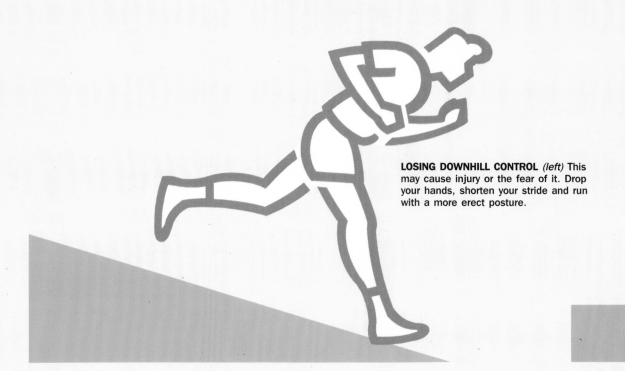

OVERSTRIDING *(right)* Do not lunge forward with your feet, but allow a natural stride. Focus on a short, fast arm swing.

LOSING DOWNHILL CONTROL *(left)* This may cause injury or the fear of it. Drop your hands, shorten your stride and run with a more erect posture.

WIDE ARM SWINGS *(left)* Keep the palms of your hands turned in and slightly up to help keep your elbows near your sides.

HUNCHED SHOULDERS *(right)* This indicates tension. Shake your shoulders and hands to loosen up and relax.

LANDING ON YOUR HEELS *(left)* Shorten your stride and increase your lean slightly, landing toward the balls of your feet.

RUNNING ON YOUR TOES *(left)* This indicates you are bouncing too high. Lean forward and lengthen your stride.

Conditioning Routines

Some runners can enhance their performance with strengthening exercises that exaggerate running form. Two of these techniques are called bounding and prancing. When you practice bounding, you leap in the air and pump your arms powerfully to create as much lift as possible. This is an exhausting exercise, but one that will strengthen your shoulders, thighs and calves.

Prancing is not quite so tiring, but requires good balance and strong abdominal muscles to perform well. Although this is an exercise to improve your running, it is actually a walk, since you always have at least one foot on the ground. To do this, rise up on your toes and walk by lifting your knees high. Land only on your toes. This exercise teaches you to keep your knees high and your legs and arms moving quickly. It also helps you to move up onto your toes when sprinting.

Use these strengthening exercises to break up your regular running routine. Start by bounding and prancing on a 30-yard stretch of grass or dirt. When you get stronger, you can progress to 100 yards. Perform these drills no more than twice a week, and never on consecutive days.

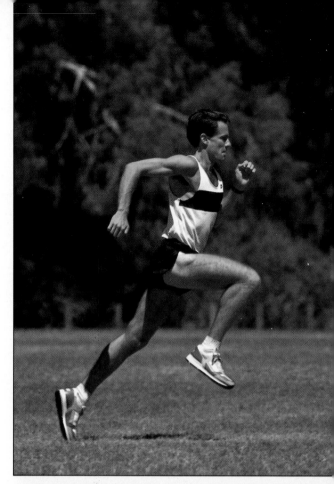

To bound, leap as high as you can with each stride *(top right)*. Pump your arms powerfully to give yourself as much lift as possible *(top center)*, and extend your legs fully, landing on your forefoot *(top, far right)*.

To prance, rise up on your toes and lift your opposite knee until your thigh is parallel to the ground *(bottom right)*. Pause briefly and then step down, again rising up on your toes *(bottom center)*. Continue walking in this manner, making sure your heels do not touch the ground *(bottom, far right)*.

Partner Running/1

Although many distance runners enjoy the solitude of their pursuit, others like company on their runs, finding that the time and the miles move quickly with a friend. Indeed, sports psychologists at Louisiana State University and the University of North Carolina found that at light and moderate levels of intensity, exercisers perceived their exertion levels to be easier when they exercised with a partner.

In addition to the psychological benefits of running with a friend, a partner can improve your motivation through friendly competition and give pointers on your technique.

Running with a partner can make fartlek running more enjoyable. Fartlek is a loosely structured form of training during which you alternately run fast or easy, depending on your mood or the terrain. While running with a partner, for instance, you can challenge each other to short races, play tag or invent other games. Fartlek runs ease your sense of exertion and increase your feelings of exhilaration and fun.

Most people find training partners entirely by happenstance; for example, you may notice someone running in a park who appears to be at your level, or perhaps a neighbor suggests that you both work out together. You can also seek training partners actively by appearing at running clubs or races and talking with other runners. However you find a partner, you can ensure the greatest benefit by choosing someone whose ability is closely matched to your own — and by following the tips presented on the next six pages.

84

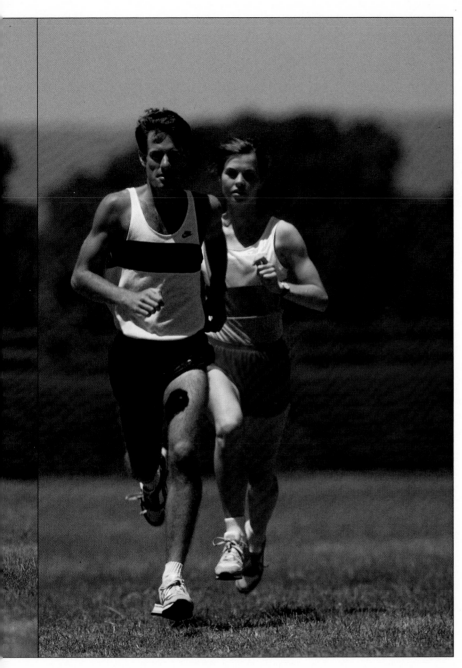

Partner Running/2

To minimize the level of exertion you perceive and still maintain a high-quality workout, do not race your partner; take turns leading. Drop a step or two behind your partner and "ride" her shoulder *(far left)*. If you look at a spot on her shoulder and match her stride, you can be "pulled" along. Trade places periodically by surging around your partner *(center)* and take the lead so that she can ride your shoulder *(left)*.

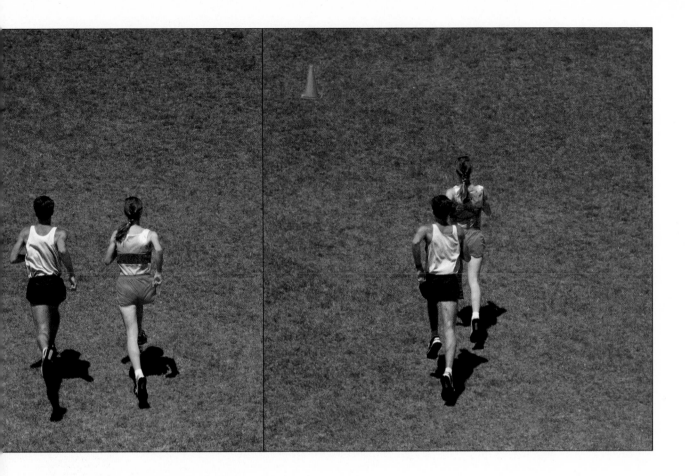

Partner Running/3

You can intensify the leading and riding technique shown on pages
84 and 85 by placing a series of cones, rocks or other markers at
varying intervals along a course or around a field. Ride your partner's
shoulder as he runs the course at a fast pace *(left)*. As you approach
one of the cones, surge ahead so that you pass your partner when you
reach the cone *(above left)*. Do not race your partner, but keep your
pace strong as he rides your shoulder. Your partner should surge
ahead at the next cone *(above right)*.

Partner Running/4

Occasionally play games with your partner to increase your enjoyment, prevent boredom and help you look forward to your next run. For instance, bring a ball with you that you can toss back and forth while you run *(below)*.

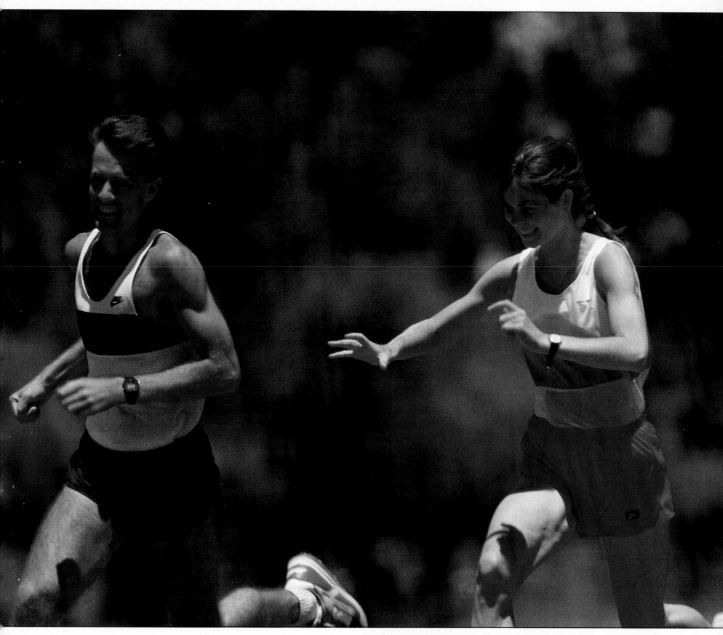

A game of tag is not only fun; it will help improve your ability to surge and sustain a sprint, either to pass someone in a race or to hold off another runner who wants to pass you *(above)*.

The Long Run

A weekly long run is the backbone of any endurance-running program; it is important for strengthening your heart and improving oxygen delivery to your working muscles. Long runs also teach your body not to rely exclusively on the glycogen stored in your muscles as an energy source: They require that you use body fat for energy, so that you not only spare some glycogen, but you burn off body fat.

Long runs also give you a psychological advantage for shorter races: If you complete a 10-mile run once a week in addition to your usual shorter runs, then completing a five-mile race will seem relatively easy.

Many runners perform a long run about once a week. In runs that may last an hour or two, many prefer to run in groups to help the time and the miles pass more quickly. Running clubs often sponsor after-work or weekend group runs of 10 to 20 miles, and runners frequently look forward to these events as social gatherings as well as endurance training. If the group is large, runners may break up into units, each one proceeding at its own pace.

Your long run should not be more than about one-third of your total weekly mileage. Plan your run in advance so that you can drink water along the route, especially in hot weather. Some runners carry water bottles with them; others prefer to carry money so they can stop to buy bottled water along the way.

Intervals

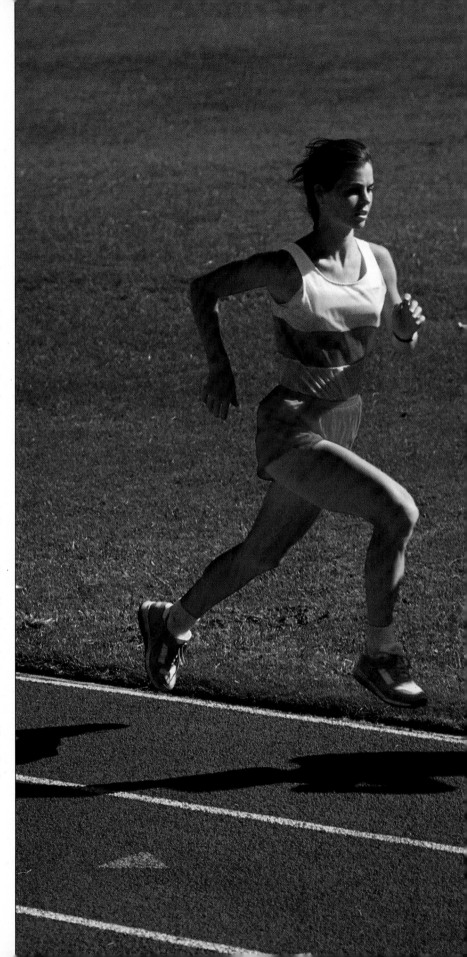

Interval training is the antithesis of the long run. Instead of endurance training over varied terrain, intervals require timed sprints over measured distances with a short recovery period between each sprint. Usually, the recovery period consists of catching your breath while you jog.

Intervals allow you to train at a higher intensity than you would normally encounter in competition. Distance runners typically perform interval training twice a week. Not only do intervals increase your speed, they also give you the mental stamina that you need in a race.

Most tracks are about a quarter mile, or 400 meters. Running on a track can put you in a mood to race, and many runners find that they run intervals too quickly. As a result, they become exhausted early in the workout, losing the benefit of interval training. Do not run each interval at an all-out pace; run each one a little faster than your normal fast pace. If you run quarter-mile intervals, for example, run each quarter at a slightly faster pace than you would run a mile.

A beginning workout may be six to eight 400-meter intervals with a 200-meter recovery jog between each. Try to run each quarter in 1:41-1:44 time. You can also run three or four 800-meter intervals with a 200-meter recovery.

As your strength and speed improve, you can cut your recovery jog time and increase the number of intervals. See the chart on pages 98-99 for a typical weekly training schedule that incorporates intervals.

Road Racing

Beginning runners most often get their first taste of road racing at distances between five kilometers (3.1 miles) and 10 kilometers (6.2 miles). The 10-kilometer, or 10-K, race has long been a staple of long-distance road running. Although marathons steal the bulk of media attention, these shorter road events are far more popular among runners. A large part of the appeal in entering five- to 10-K races is that many people routinely train about three to six miles for them.

Training for and running five- to 10-K races are likely to increase your aerobic capacity. Studies show that the oxygen consumption of top-ranked athletes during a five-K race is about 98 percent of their maximum, while those running a 10-K race use about 90 percent. If you im-

prove your oxygen consumption by running these races, then your performance is likely to improve.

Whatever distance you run for your first race, you should not be concerned with your finishing time. Concentrate on enjoying yourself and completing the race. Perhaps when you enter your second race, you can better your time. In that case, wear a watch and keep track of mile markers if the course has them. Then you can gauge your pace, the distance you have covered and the distance remaining, so that you can expend your energy accordingly. If the course does not have mile markers, use your usual training pace as a guide to determine how far you have run after a specific elapsed time. (Realize that you will probably run faster when you race.)

The Marathon

No other running experience equals that of competing in a marathon, the grueling 26.2-mile endurance race. Runners frequently aspire to a marathon either as the goal or the high point of their training.

Long considered the limit of human endurance, the marathon taxes the strength and stamina of even the most highly trained athlete. To be minimally in shape to complete a marathon, you should run at least 40 miles a week for six weeks, and have run at least two 20-mile training runs. In addition, you should run several shorter races, from three to 15 or 20 miles, to gain experience before attempting a marathon.

The week before the race, taper off your training, and jog lightly the day prior to the marathon. On the morning of the race, have a light, bland breakfast of dry toast and juice. Arrive at the start at least an hour early to check in, stretch and warm up. Be sure to bring petroleum jelly to rub on the inside of your thighs, feet and other places where friction may cause chafing or blisters. Pack extra shoelaces, another pair of running shoes, safety pins for fastening your race number to your jersey and dry clothing to wear after the race. Double knot your shoelaces before the race.

The eight pages that follow give you guidelines and tips on actually running various portions of a race; you can apply this advice to running a marathon as well as to competing in shorter-distance events.

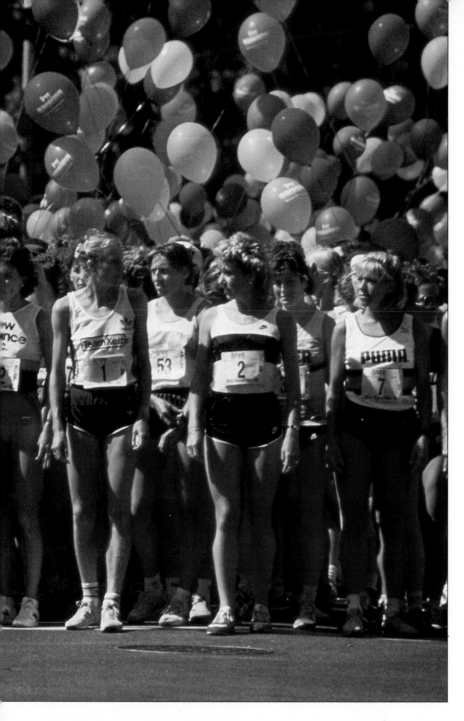

Starting the Race

The first step in a running event is deciding where your starting position should be. If you stand at the front, it is likely that faster runners will push you aside. If you start at the rear, you will spend much energy just running around other people.

In crowded races, unless you are an elite athlete and deserve to stand in the front line, it is best to stay at a spot in the middle of the field. Then you can pick up your pace during the race when the congestion thins out, rather than risk tripping or bumping into someone at the start.

Do not begin the race with a sprint; aim for a strong, steady pace. By the 1.5-mile point in a six-mile race, you should have found a pace that will carry you through most of the distance. In a marathon, it may take you as long as six miles to find your pace.

Maintaining Your Pace

Theoretically, the perfect race consists of even splits — meaning that each mile is run at exactly the same pace — and a fast finish. Few races follow a predetermined plan, however. Instead, you will likely find tactical reasons to speed up or slow down at various portions of the race, according to how you feel and what conditions, including other runners, are present.

Once you have found your pace (*see page 99*), you may want to run in a small group. Settle in with a group that wants to finish the race in about the same time you do. You may find yourself matching other runners' strides step for step, and you may even feel yourself pulled along by them as you run.

Another benefit of running in a group is that you can use the others to build your own confidence. Listen to their breathing and talk to them briefly to gauge how they feel. One runner may dominate the group and set the pace. Ride this leader's shoulder, if you feel you can keep up, or stay just a half step behind. When the leader surges, follow him; you can use his speed to spur your own. Or, if you have the capability, leave the pack of runners behind and enter a faster group, or run by yourself, aware that the pack is following you.

Water Stops

Virtually all races of six miles or longer feature water stops. While a six-mile race may offer water only at the halfway point and the finish, large urban marathons frequently boast water tables every two miles. It is important during a race, particularly in races longer than six miles, to drink water whenever possible. On a hot day, you should drink even if you are not thirsty; otherwise, you will very likely become dehydrated.

Drinking on the run is an art that takes practice to perfect. Take the water cup in one hand and squeeze it gently to form a spout. Then raise it to your lips and take short sips.

If you cannot drink and run at the same time, then stop for a moment and drink. Some runners also take a cup of water and pour it over their heads. The water on your head may feel great for a few seconds, but it will not cool you down. Studies show that even water sprays are not sufficient to reduce your core body temperature while you run. Only drinking cool water at regular intervals will prevent dehydration.

The Finish

If you want to make a strong finish, do not wait until you see the finish line to kick into a sprint. If you do, chances are you will be outkicked.

When other runners are tiring toward the end of the race, use your arms to pump and pick up your pace. Increase your pace at the four-mile point of a six-mile race. In a marathon, pick up your pace with a mile to go, so your time will be faster and you will have a better chance of breaking away from other runners.

Once you cross the finish line, jog slowly or walk to cool down. If the weather is the least bit cool, be sure to keep moving and put on warm clothing as soon as possible. Drink water or fruit juice. Although some runners enjoy drinking beer after races, it is better to avoid all alcoholic drinks until you are completely rehydrated, since alcohol is a diuretic that can increase dehydration.

Part of finishing every race is the recovery period, which may last for days or even weeks after a particularly strenuous race. Runners often become injured by returning to their normal workouts too soon after a race. Take it easy for the first day or two, and exercise moderately if you feel particularly sore and stiff. Jog, bicycle, swim or walk briskly until your legs recover from the race, and stretch frequently.

Run half your usual mileage for the first week after a race, then increase the distance gradually during the second week. If you enter races as part of your regular training, you may be able to race two or three times a month. However, do not attempt to run two marathons in less than three months.

Training to Race

For your first race or two, you may only be interested in enjoying the experience and completing the distance. During additional races, however, you may want to improve your time.

If you are just starting out, begin your training slowly, as outlined on pages 20-21. Comprehensive studies by Soviet researchers have proved that no one system of training — intervals, hill work, fartlek, or endurance running — is most effective for race training. The best approach is to utilize all of these techniques. The schedule shown at right outlines a general plan that includes distance running and interval work.

To adopt the greatest variety of training techniques, most schedules utilize the principle of alternating hard and easy workouts. If you run hard intervals on Tuesday, for instance, run an easy eight to 10 miles on Wednesday. Likewise, if you run hills or fartlek one day, perform a long, steady run the following day.

In addition to running alternate hard and easy days, many competitive runners employ double workouts on some of their hard days. A double workout incorporates two training sessions; for example, a long, slow run in the morning and track intervals in the early evening.

Keep in mind that every runner is different. The schedule at right is only an example and not necessarily one that you should follow strictly. For best results, you should consult a coach or experienced competitor to help you devise an optimal schedule that fits your goals.

MONDAY

TUESDAY

WEDNESDAY

THURSDAY

FRIDAY

SATURDAY

SUNDAY

	WEEK *1*	WEEK *2*	WEEK *3*	WEEK *4*
	10 mi.	10 mi.	10 mi.	10 mi.
A.M. **P.M.**	8 mi. 15 × 440 yd.	6 × 1 mi. 8 mi.	8 mi. 15 × 440 yd.	7 × 1 mi. 8 mi.
	8 mi.	10 mi.	8 mi.	10 mi.
A.M. **P.M.**	6 mi. 10 × 880 yd.	4 × 1.5 mi. 6 mi.	6 mi. 10 × 880 yd.	5 × 1.5 mi. 6 mi.
	6 mi.	4 mi.	6 mi.	6 mi.
	8 mi.	6 mi.	8 mi.	4 mi.
	OFF	OFF	OFF	**RACE**

If your track is measured in meters, 440 yards = 400 meters; 880 yards = 800 meters.

CHAPTER FOUR

Strength Conditioning

A program for walkers and runners

Even if you walk or run five miles a day or more, you are probably not doing all you can to develop your overall fitness. Although walking and running are excellent cardiovascular conditioners — and they certainly develop the powerful muscles of your thighs, calves and buttocks — they do not exercise your upper body. Traditionally, competitive walkers and runners believe that nothing conditions their bodies better than simply more walking and running. However, inspired by the success of elite athletes who have incorporated weight training into their programs, more and more competitors and fitness enthusiasts alike are discovering the benefits of upper body workouts. By developing your muscle strength and joint stability, weight training can increase your endurance and speed, help prevent injuries and improve your posture.

The upper body does far more than just provide the lower body with a stable hinge from which the legs can swing back and forth. Studies show that the arms and shoulders not only help balance the body in motion, but contribute to as much as 10 percent of a runner's vertical lift. This additional lift gives the runner more "flight" time, so that his foot stride is extended considerably and his running speed is increased. The more powerfully the arms pump, therefore, the faster the running speed.

Strong arms and shoulders are also important for walking, though for different reasons. Because at least one foot is always in contact with the ground when you walk, your arms do not contribute to vertical lift. In casual walking, the arms and shoulders act simply to counterbalance the swinging motion of the legs. However, as your walking speed increases, so does the contribution of your upper body. When you race walk, your shoulder and arm swings transmit torque and power to the hips, contributing up to 50 percent of the propulsive force of your stride. Arm and shoulder movement also helps keep you "on track," that is, moving forward along a straight line without unnecessary side-to-side weight shifts.

To test the importance of your arms and shoulders to your walking speed, try walking as fast as you can while you keep your shoulders rigid and your arms at your sides. Then race walk, pumping your arms and shoulders powerfully: You will notice that not only is it easier to walk with your arms and shoulders moving, but that your stride length, cadence and walking speed will increase.

A good walker or runner must utilize the dynamic contribution that the upper body can make to endurance, speed and stride. To do so, you should develop your upper body to complement your lower body training. According to exercise physiologists, the more closely your strength conditioning reflects the activity for which you are training, the more effective it will be. This is called the principle of specificity. Following this concept, many of the exercise routines in this chapter mimic body postures and movements you use frequently in your normal daily walking and running workouts.

Moreover, for maximum effectiveness, your weight-training program should target the same types of muscle fibers that your regular workout exercises. Sprinters, for instance, are concerned with strength and speed. Physiologists know that top-ranked sprinters have highly developed fast-twitch muscle fibers, which are recruited for sudden bursts of power. Since working out with heavy weights selectively trains the fast-twitch muscle fibers, many sprinters incorporate weight-training exercises in their routines.

The muscles of elite marathon runners and race walkers, in contrast, contain slow-twitch fibers predominantly, which are used for endurance exercise. Lifting lighter weights repeatedly develops slow-twitch muscle fibers. If you are a fitness walker or a distance runner, and you want to improve your performance, you should not be working out with heavy weights. Instead, weight train with poundages somewhat below your maximum capacity, repeating each exercise 20 to 40 times. By performing many repetitions, or reps, which will closely parallel your fitness-walking or endurance-running programs, you

Working Out with Weights

◆ To warm up before you lift weights, walk briskly, jog in place or jump rope for five to 10 minutes. Warming up will improve your muscle and joint range of motion and help reduce the chance of sustaining an injury.

◆ Train with free weights no more than three times a week, with at least one day of rest between workouts. This will prevent overtraining, which can result in muscle fatigue, soreness and injury.

◆ Keep track of your progress on a chart or in a journal. Be sure to indicate the exercises you perform, the weights you lift and the number of repetitions in each set. When you note that you can lift a particular weight for more than your usual number of reps for two or three consecutive workout sessions, graduate to a heavier weight.

◆ With experience, you should be able to judge how much to increase the effort in order to gear your weight training to your walking or running. If you are running strictly for distance, for instance, you may wish to increase your reps to 40 or more. If you are running to increase your speed, or if you are increasing your hill work, cut back on the number of reps and increase the amount of weight you lift. To work on both strength and endurance, weight train in sets of 10 reps. Perform 10 reps, pause, then perform two more sets of 10 reps. You should lift enough weight so that by the tenth rep of the final set, you are too exhausted to perform another rep.

will develop your slow-twitch fibers — with some crossover benefit to your fast-twitch fibers.

Train your muscles by using the technique of progressive resistance. Since your muscles adapt to the stress you place on them, they grow stronger only if you increase the demand progressively. You can do this by increasing the number of reps to improve muscle endurance, or by increasing the amount of weight to develop muscle strength. In this way, you can fine-tune your weight-training program to complement your regular workouts (*see the box above*).

If you are a distance runner, you need not worry that weight training will develop muscle bulk so much that it interferes with efficient running: The slow-twitch fibers targeted by using lighter weight and many reps do not increase in size substantially. Your upper body muscles will maintain moderate mass even though their endurance capacity increases.

You can perform your workout at home or in a gym. However, you may find that exercising at home is the most convenient and least expensive alternative. All you need to start are a set of dumbbells, an exercise bench and a mat. You can lift weights in your usual exercise attire, but be sure to wear enough clothing to keep warm; cold muscles are less flexible and tend to become injured more easily than warm muscles. Warm up for five to 10 minutes before you begin to lift weights; cool down for the same amount of time afterward.

Upper Body Routine/1

To build your upper body, perform a routine with dumbbells, an exercise bench and a floor mat. This chapter provides a complete conditioning regimen to strengthen all the major muscles in your upper body. Like most routines, it starts with the larger muscles of the upper back and chest, then progresses to the smaller muscles. This order will help prevent fatigue. Since this routine is designed for walkers and runners specifically, it incorporates unilateral swinging motions of the upper arms and shoulders whenever possible, to mimic walking and running arm motions and positions.

Unless otherwise indicated, perform one set of 20 to 30 repetitions for each exercise, or follow the guidelines in the box on page 111. Lift weights that are heavy enough so that your muscles will be exhausted temporarily at the end of each set, but not so heavy that you are unable to complete the set. If a routine shows an exercise for one side of your body, be sure to repeat the same exercise for the other side. Perform these exercises two or three times a week, with at least one rest day between workouts.

Perform pullovers to strengthen your upper back. Lie face up on an exercise bench. Hold a dumbbell in your left hand, and bring it over and behind your head, until you feel a stretch in your chest *(top left)*. Keep your elbow bent slightly and lift the weight over your chest *(left center)*. Lower the dumbbell to your abdomen *(left)* and return to the starting position.

Perform bent-over rows to strengthen your back and upper arms. Bend over an exercise bench and support yourself with your left hand. Hold a dumbbell in your right hand *(above)*. Lift the dumbbell straight up to your chest *(above right)* and then lower it to the starting position.

To strengthen your lower back muscles, lie face down on an exercise mat with your arms at your sides. Raise your chest and shoulders off the floor, keeping your pelvis in place *(right)*. Return slowly to the starting position.

Upper Body
Routine/2

Perform a dumbbell bench press to work
your chest, shoulders and triceps. Lie face
up on an exercise bench and hold two
dumbbells just a little wider than shoulder-
width apart *(right)*. Simultaneously press
the dumbbells straight up without locking
your elbows *(far right)*. Return to the starting position.

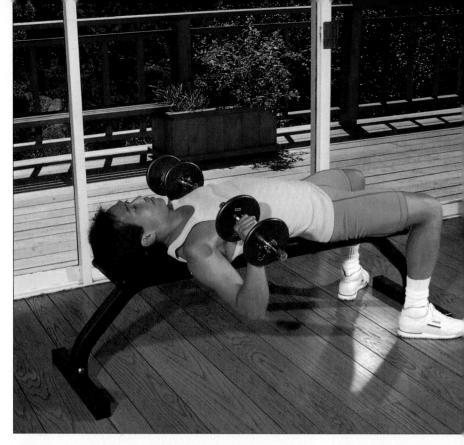

A bent-arm fly is similar to the bench
press. Without locking your elbows, raise
two dumbbells over your chest *(right)*.
Lower your arms to your sides until you
feel a stretch in your chest *(far right)*.
Return to the starting position.

Upper Body Routine/3

Perform lateral arm raises to strengthen your shoulders. Stand erect with your knees bent slightly, while holding the dumbbells at your sides. Raise the dumbbells laterally until your arms are parallel to the floor *(below)*. Return to the starting position to complete one repetition.

Perform single-arm raises to further strengthen your shoulders. Hold the dumbbells at your sides and stand with your knees bent slightly. Keeping your elbow bent, raise your right arm in front of you until the dumbbell is at shoulder height *(above)*. Lower your right arm; raise and lower your left arm in the same manner *(above right)*.

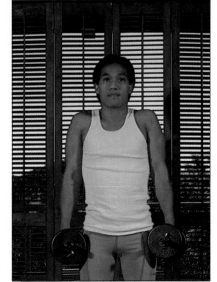

You can also perform shoulder shrugs for your trapezius muscles. Stand erect and hold the dumbbells at your sides. Lift your shoulders straight up *(right)*; then return to the starting position.

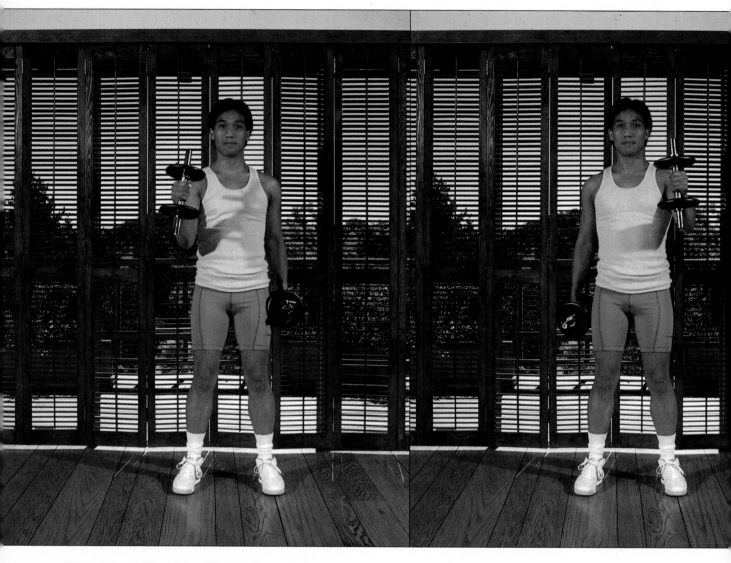

Upper Body Routine/4

Perform arm curls to strengthen your biceps muscles. Stand erect with your knees bent slightly, and hold the dumbbells at your sides. Bend your right elbow and raise the dumbbell to chest level *(above)*. Return to the starting position, and repeat for your left biceps *(above right)*.

To perform triceps extensions, bend over an exercise bench and support yourself with your right hand. Hold a dumbbell in your left hand, but keep your upper arm and elbow next to your body *(left)*. Keeping your upper arm in the same position, extend your lower arm *(below left)*. Return to the starting position.

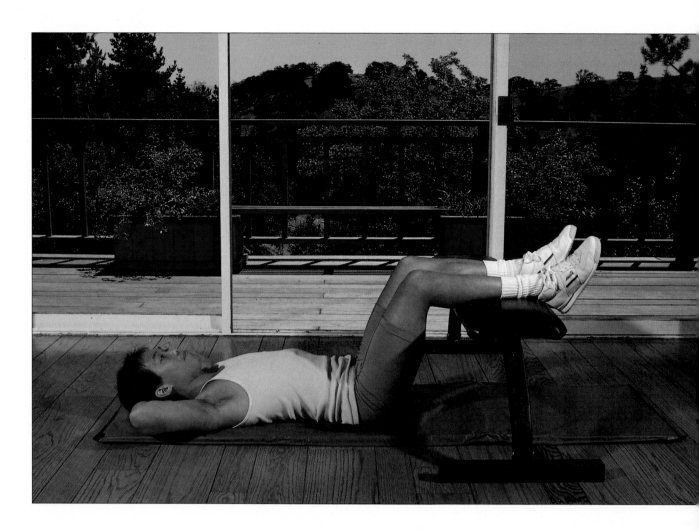

Upper Body Routine/5

Perform bent-knee crunches to strengthen your abdominals. Lie face up on a mat with your hands behind your head and your lower legs supported on an exercise bench *(above)*. Tighten your abdominals and raise your head, shoulders and upper back off the floor *(opposite)*. Return to the starting position.

To increase the intensity of the bent-knee crunch shown above, hold a light weight disk behind your head and perform the same exercise *(right)*.

121

Upper Body Routine/6

Perform lateral side bends to strengthen and stretch your sides and the muscles between your ribs. Stand erect with your knees bent slightly and your right hand behind your head *(above left)*, holding a dumbbell with your left hand. Bend to the left, allowing the weight of the dumbbell to pull your left arm and shoulder toward the floor *(above)*. Return to the starting position.

Perform crossover sit-ups for your obliques, or side muscles. Lie on your back, place your hands behind your head and cross your right foot over your left knee *(above left)*. Keeping your right elbow on the floor, raise your left shoulder and upper back *(left)*. Return to the starting position.

CHAPTER FIVE

The Right Diet

Quality nutrients — and convenient recipes — to enhance endurance

The most important fuel for walking and running — as for all activity requiring endurance — is food rich in complex carbohydrates. This nutrient, which is derived from cereals, grains, fruits and vegetables, supplies at least 50 percent of the energy you need for moderate activity. When you are very active, this percentage increases significantly: A person who runs at 75 percent of his VO_2max, for example, derives nearly all of his energy from stored carbohydrates. In fact, studies have shown repeatedly that athletes on a high-carbohydrate diet have three times the endurance of athletes on a diet high in fat. Although fat can also be a source of energy, food rich in fat can be metabolized easily only in the presence of carbohydrates. A very small amount of energy comes from protein; its primary function is to build and repair cells and tissues. And carbohydrates are also necessary for the regulation of protein metabolism in the body.

All carbohydrates are composed of sugars. Simple sugars include fructose and glucose from fruits and vegetables; sucrose, refined from sugar cane or sugar beets; and lactose, or milk sugar. These sugars are broken down to their simplest form, absorbed in the small intestine during digestion and converted by the body into glucose, the form of sugar found in the bloodstream. Your body uses some of this sugar to maintain a constant level in the blood, since your cells must take sugar from the bloodstream for energy. A small amount of the excess is stored in the liver and muscles in the form of glycogen, which can be reconverted to usable glucose for the cells, and the rest goes to form body fat.

Complex carbohydrates, as long chains of sugars are known, are derived from plant starches and from the fiber that forms the outer shell of grains and other plant foods. Ultimately, the starches are broken down into glucose — just as the simple sugars are. The body can store only a small amount of these sugars as glycogen — to a maximum of 1,500 calories, or about three quarters of a pound — and any excess calories in complex carbohydrates will be stored as body fat. Recent research has suggested that calories derived from fat are more likely to become body fat than those derived from complex carbohydrates, but these findings are still considered controversial.

Body fat is the primary way that animals store energy; each pound of fat contains 4,200 calories, of which 3,500 can be used for fuel. In comparison, plants store energy as carbohydrates, and each pound of carbohydrates contains 1,700 calories, of which a much smaller percentage can be used for fuel than calories stored as fat. (Carbohydrates also form fiber in plants. When this fiber is part of your food, it is generally not metabolized, but passes through the body more or less unchanged.) While fat is a much more efficient energy-storage medium, it is metabolized at a significantly slower rate than carbohydrates. Endurance athletes depend on carbohydrates as an important exercise fuel for this reason. And since carbohydrates cannot be stored in large amounts, exercisers must replace what they use by eating food rich in carbohydrates.

Foods high in complex carbohydrates not only fuel endurance, but are also often nutritionally rich. Many of them contain protein, and they are almost always high in vitamins and minerals, which makes them a better choice than foods high in fat or simple sugars. In recent years, most nutritionists have come to believe that consuming 55 percent of your total calories mostly in the form of complex carbohydrates is the healthiest way to eat. You should derive a maximum of 30 percent of your calories from fats, and the remaining 15 percent of your calories from protein sources. (The headnotes that accompany the recipes in this chapter point out some of the nutritional bonuses of the high-carbohydrate foods that are recommended.)

Studies have shown that eating complex carbohydrates soon after exercise is an effective way to replace muscle glycogen. Some researchers believe that endurance athletes can also benefit from a

The Basic Guidelines

For a moderately active adult, the National Institutes of Health recommends a diet that is low in fat, high in carbohydrates and moderate in protein. The institutes' guidelines suggest that no more than 30 percent of your calories come from fat, that 55 percent to 60 percent come from carbohydrates and that no more than 15 percent come from protein. A gram of fat equals nine calories, while a gram of protein or carbohydrate equals four calories; therefore, if you eat 2,100 calories a day, you should consume approximately 60 grams of fat, 315 grams of carbohydrate and no more than 75 grams of protein daily. If you follow a lowfat/high-carbohydrate diet, your chance of developing heart disease, cancer and other life-threatening diseases may be considerably reduced.

◆ The nutrition charts that accompany each of the lowfat/high-carbohydrate recipes in this book include the number of calories per serving, the number of grams of fat, carbohydrate and protein in a serving, and the percentage of calories derived from each of these nutrients. In addition, the charts provide the amount of calcium, iron and sodium per serving.

◆ Calcium deficiency may be associated with periodontal disease — which attacks the mouth's bones and tissues, including the gums — in both men and women, and with osteoporosis, or bone shrinking and weakening, in the elderly. The deficiency may also contribute to high blood pressure. The recommended daily allowance for calcium is 800 milligrams a day for men and women. Pregnant and lactating women are advised to consume 1,200 milligrams daily; a National Institutes of Health consensus panel recommends that postmenopausal women consume 1,200 to 1,500 milligrams of calcium each day.

◆ Although one way you can reduce your fat intake is to cut your consumption of red meat, you should make sure that you get your necessary iron from other sources. The Food and Nutrition Board of the National Academy of Sciences suggests a minimum of 10 milligrams of iron per day for men and 18 milligrams for women between the ages of 11 and 50.

◆ High sodium intake is associated with high blood pressure. Most adults should restrict sodium intake to between 2,000 and 2,500 milligrams a day, according to the National Academy of Sciences. One way to keep sodium consumption in check is not to add table salt to food.

diet technique called carbohydrate loading, which entails eating considerably more than the recommended 55 percent of carbohydrates before a competition. But this regimen has been shown to be effective, if at all, only for exercise that lasts for a minimum of 90 minutes, when muscle glycogen is depleted.

This chapter presents recipes that generally supply more than 55 percent of carbohydrates. They do not comprise a balanced diet by themselves, but help to boost your carbohydrate intake as you eat properly. The legumes, rice, pasta, fruits and vegetables included here are all low in fat. If you are embarking on a walking or running program, or if you compete in either activity, you will benefit from including these recipes in your diet. And since, by weight, carbohydrates have the same number of calories as proteins but fewer than half the calories of fats, a high-carbohydrate/lowfat diet makes weight control relatively easy to accomplish.

Hominy-Currant Muffins

Breakfast

. . . .

HOMINY-CURRANT MUFFINS

A cinnamon-raisin Danish contains about 40 percent more fat and 30 percent less carbohydrates than one of these muffins.

CALORIES per muffin	171
80% Carbohydrate	35 g
10% Protein	4 g
10% Fat	2 g
CALCIUM	77 mg
IRON	2 mg
SODIUM	242 mg

1/3 cup instant grits
1 1/4 cups unbleached
   all-purpose flour
1 cup yellow cornmeal
3 tablespoons sugar
2 teaspoons baking powder
3/4 teaspoon baking soda

1/4 teaspoon salt
1 egg
1 cup skim milk
1 tablespoon margarine, melted
   and cooled
1 cup dried currants

Preheat the oven to 400° F. Bring a small saucepan of water to a boil. Meanwhile, line 12 muffin tin cups with paper liners; set aside. Place the grits in a small bowl, add 1/2 cup of boiling water and stir until blended; set aside. In a medium-size bowl stir together the flour, cornmeal, sugar, baking powder, baking soda and salt, and make a well in the center; set aside. Beat the egg in a small bowl, then stir in the milk and margarine. Pour the egg mixture and the grits into the dry ingredients and stir briefly, then add the currants and stir just until combined. Divide the batter among the muffin tins (they will be nearly full) and bake for 25 minutes, or until the muffins are golden brown on top and a toothpick inserted in the center of a muffin comes out clean and dry.

Makes 12 muffins

BLUEBERRY COBBLER

The carbohydrates in the fruit and crust will keep your energy level high, while the minimal amount of fat in the crust keeps this breakfast from "weighing you down" all morning long.

Vegetable cooking spray

2 cups fresh or frozen blueberries

3 tablespoons maple syrup

1/2 cup unbleached all-purpose flour, approximately

3/4 teaspoon baking powder

1/2 teaspoon ground cinnamon

1/8 teaspoon salt

1 tablespoon plus 1 1/2 teaspoons margarine, melted

1 tablespoon skim milk

1 teaspoon grated lemon peel

CALORIES per serving	178
71% Carbohydrate	32 g
5% Protein	2 g
24% Fat	5 g
CALCIUM	73 mg
IRON	1 mg
SODIUM	208 mg

Preheat the oven to 400° F. Lightly spray a 9-inch pie plate with cooking spray; set aside. If using fresh berries, wash, dry, stem and pick them over. Combine the blueberries and maple syrup in a small saucepan and cook over medium heat, stirring occasionally, for 5 minutes, or until the berries are very soft; remove the pan from the heat and set aside.

Combine 1/2 cup of flour, the baking powder, cinnamon and salt in a medium-size bowl and stir to combine. Stir in the margarine, milk and lemon peel, and mix until a soft dough forms. Turn the dough onto a lightly floured surface and roll it out with a floured rolling pin to a 9-inch round about 1/8 inch thick. Stir the berry mixture, pour it into the pie plate and lay the crust on top. Bake the cobbler for 25 minutes. Let it cool for 5 minutes before serving, then cut it in quarters and serve warm. 　　　　　　　　　　　Makes 4 servings

FRENCH TOAST WITH RASPBERRY-ORANGE SAUCE

The glucose in whole grains is released more slowly than that in refined products, making whole-wheat bread a superior fuel for the athlete.

3/4 cup skim milk

1/4 cup orange juice

1 1/2 teaspoons grated orange peel

2 eggs

1/2 teaspoon ground cinnamon

1/4 teaspoon ground nutmeg

8 slices whole-wheat bread

3 cups fresh or frozen raspberries (1 pint)

2 tablespoons brown sugar

1 tablespoon plus 1 1/2 teaspoons margarine

8 orange segments for garnish

CALORIES per serving	318
62% Carbohydrate	52 g
14% Protein	12 g
24% Fat	9 g
CALCIUM	176 mg
IRON	3 mg
SODIUM	353 mg

In a medium-size bowl whisk together the milk, orange juice and peel, eggs, cinnamon and nutmeg. Lay the bread slices in a large baking pan and pour the milk mixture over them, turning the bread once to coat it with the mixture; set aside for 20 minutes. Tilt the pan occasionally to enable the bread to absorb all the liquid. Meanwhile, combine the raspberries and sugar in a food processor or blender and process until puréed. Strain the purée through a sieve, then transfer it to a small pitcher and set aside.

Melt half the margarine in a large nonstick skillet over medium-high heat. Add 4 slices of bread and cook for 4 minutes on each side, or until golden brown. Melt the remaining margarine in the skillet and cook the remaining bread in the same fashion. Divide the French toast among 4 plates, top each serving with sauce and garnish with orange segments. 　　Makes 4 servings

RAISIN BUTTERMILK WAFFLES WITH STRAWBERRY PUREE

CALORIES per serving	243
65% Carbohydrate	40 g
11% Protein	7 g
24% Fat	7 g
CALCIUM	113 mg
IRON	2 mg
SODIUM	218 mg

In addition to providing 40 grams of carbohydrates, these fruit-topped waffles supply good amounts of vitamin C, calcium and potassium, all important nutrients for athletes. Vitamin C assists in the conservation of glycogen, the body's main muscle fuel, thereby enhancing endurance. Calcium acts in concert with exercise like walking and running to build strong, dense bones. Potassium helps regulate the body's water balance and is involved in energy release within the muscles; insufficient potassium can cause muscle weakness and cramping during exercise.

1 1/2 cups fresh or unsweetened frozen strawberries

1 1/2 teaspoons confectioners' sugar, or less to taste

1 egg, separated

2/3 cups buttermilk

1 tablespoon plus 1 1/2 teaspoons margarine, melted and cooled

1 cup unbleached all-purpose flour

1 1/2 teaspoons granulated sugar

3/4 teaspoon baking powder

1/8 teaspoon baking soda

1/4 cup dark raisins

Vegetable cooking spray (optional)

If using fresh strawberries, wash, dry and hull them. If using frozen berries, thaw them just enough to separate them, then drain and pat them dry. For the strawberry purée, combine half the berries with 3/4 teaspoon of confectioners' sugar in a food processor or blender and process for about 1 minute, or until smoothly puréed. Slice the remaining berries and set them aside separately.

Preheat the oven to 200° F. Preheat a nonstick waffle iron. (If your waffle iron does not have a nonstick surface, spray it with cooking spray before preheating it. Do not respray the hot waffle iron.) In a small bowl whisk together the egg yolk, buttermilk and margarine until blended; set aside. In a large bowl combine the flour, granulated sugar, baking powder and baking soda and stir until well mixed; set aside. In a medium-size bowl, using an electric mixer, beat the egg white until it is stiff but not dry. Add the buttermilk mixture to the dry ingredients and stir until blended, then stir in the raisins. Using a rubber spatula, gently fold in the egg white.

Pour about 2/3 cup of batter into the center of the waffle iron, spread it evenly with the rubber spatula, and cook for 5 minutes, or according to the manufacturer's instructions, until the waffle is golden. Place it on a heatproof platter, cover it loosely with foil and place it in the oven to keep warm. Make another waffle in the same fashion. Divide each large waffle into four, place 2 small waffles on each of 4 plates and top each serving with one fourth of the sauce. Arrange the sliced strawberries on top, sprinkle the waffles with the remaining confectioners' sugar and serve.   Makes 4 servings

Bean and Tuna Salad

Lunch
· · · · · · · · · · · ·

BEAN AND TUNA SALAD

The beans in this salad provide more than 4 grams of protein—and virtually no fat—as well as slowly released glucose for lasting energy.

CALORIES per serving	310
61% Carbohydrate	47 g
17% Protein	13 g
22% Fat	8 g
CALCIUM	107 mg
IRON	4 mg
SODIUM	384 mg

6 tablespoons lemon juice

2 tablespoons olive oil

2 tablespoons chopped
   fresh parsley

1 teaspoon chopped fresh
   rosemary, or 1/4 teaspoon
   dried rosemary

1/4 teaspoon black pepper

Pinch of salt

2 cups diced carrots

1 1/2 cups coarsely chopped
   scallions

1 cup diced celery

1 cup cooked white beans,
   rinsed and drained if canned

1 1/2 ounces water-packed
   white tuna (about 1/4 of a
   7-ounce can)

6 ounces French bread

12 large Boston lettuce leaves

For the dressing, in a small bowl whisk together the lemon juice, oil, parsley, rosemary, pepper and salt. In a large bowl toss together the carrots, scallions and celery. If using canned beans, rinse them under cold running water and drain them; drain the tuna. Add the beans and tuna to the salad, pour the dressing over it and toss it gently. Let the salad stand at room temperature for at least 30 minutes, or refrigerate it for at least 2 hours. Meanwhile, wash and dry the lettuce. To serve, line 4 plates with lettuce leaves and spoon the tuna salad on top; serve the bread alongside.   Makes 4 servings

STUFFED MUSHROOM BAKE

Many casserole recipes call for sodium-laden canned soup and lots of high-fat cheese. This dish is made with a fresh tomato sauce, just a touch of salt and a mere sprinkling of cheese.

8 very large fresh mushrooms
1 tablespoon olive oil
5 cups coarsely chopped onions
2 tablespoons low-sodium
   chicken stock
3 garlic cloves, minced
1 teaspoon each chopped
   fresh thyme and rosemary, or
   1/2 teaspoon each dried

1/2 teaspoon salt
1/4 teaspoon black pepper
1 1/2 cups cooked brown rice
   (1/2 cup raw)
2 1/4 cups diced fresh tomatoes
1/4 cup chopped fresh basil, or
   1 teaspoon dried
2 tablespoons grated Parmesan

Preheat the oven to 350° F. Wash the mushrooms and remove and chop the stems; set aside. Heat the oil in a medium-size skillet over medium heat. Add the mushroom caps, hollow side up, and sauté for 3 minutes. Transfer the mushroom caps to a plate and set aside. Add the mushroom stems, half of the onions, 1 tablespoon of stock, the garlic, thyme, rosemary, 1/4 teaspoon of salt and the pepper to the skillet. Cook, stirring, for 5 minutes, then add the rice and cook for 3 minutes more. Transfer the rice mixture to a bowl.

For the tomato sauce, heat the remaining stock in the skillet, add the remaining onions and cook, stirring, for 5 minutes. Add the tomatoes, basil and remaining salt, and cook, stirring, for 5 minutes more.

Spoon half of the tomato sauce into the bottom of an 8-inch square baking pan and spoon 3/4 cup of the rice mixture on top. Lay the mushroom caps, hollow side up, on the rice and spoon the remaining rice mixture over and around them. Pour the remaining tomato sauce over the mushrooms and sprinkle them with Parmesan. Cover the pan tightly with foil and bake for 15 minutes, or until heated through.

Makes 4 servings

CALORIES per serving	209
66% Carbohydrate	36 g
12% Protein	7 g
22% Fat	5 g
CALCIUM	102 mg
IRON	3 mg
SODIUM	336 mg

CHICKEN-NOODLE SOUP WITH VEGETABLES

The body requires more of the B vitamins thiamine and riboflavin during strenuous exercise. These vitamins, abundantly supplied by enriched pasta, play a crucial role in the body's production of energy from dietary carbohydrates and fats.

2 tablespoons olive oil
2 1/2 cups diced carrots
1 1/2 cups chopped scallions
1 green bell pepper, seeded
   and diced
3 cups low-sodium
   chicken stock

6 ounces linguine
1/3 cup chopped fresh parsley
2 tablespoons chopped fresh dill,
   or 2 teaspoons dried
1/2 teaspoon salt
1/2 teaspoon black pepper

Heat the oil in a medium-size skillet over medium heat. Add the carrots, scallions and bell pepper, and sauté for 4 minutes, or until the carrots are softened. Add the stock and 1 cup of water and bring the mixture to a simmer.

CALORIES per serving	197
62% Carbohydrate	31 g
12% Protein	6 g
26% Fat	6 g
CALCIUM	52 mg
IRON	3 mg
SODIUM	234 mg

Break the linguine into 2-inch lengths and stir it into the soup. When the soup returns to a simmer, stir in the parsley, dill, salt, pepper, and cook for another 10 minutes, or until the linguine is al dente. Ladle the soup into 6 bowls and serve immediately.   Makes 6 servings

MINESTRONE

Hot soup is welcome after a cold-weather walk or run: It warms the body while replenishing depleted fluids and carbohydrates. This home-made soup contains only about half the sodium of canned minestrone and about five times as much potassium.

CALORIES per serving	307
71% Carbohydrate	57 g
20% Protein	16 g
9% Fat	3 g
CALCIUM	108 mg
IRON	6 mg
SODIUM	471 mg

Three 10 1/2-ounce cans
   low-sodium chicken stock
3 1/2 cups peeled, diced potatoes
2 cups diced fresh tomatoes
1 1/2 cups diced zucchini
1 cup cooked kidney beans,
   rinsed and drained if canned

1 cup diced carrots
1/2 cup chopped fresh parsley
2 tablespoons tomato paste
1 garlic clove, minced
1/2 teaspoon salt
1/4 teaspoon pepper
2 tablespoons grated Parmesan

Bring the stock to a boil in a large saucepan over medium-high heat. Add the potatoes, reduce the heat to medium and cook for 15 minutes, or until the potatoes are barely tender. Add the tomatoes, zucchini, beans, carrots, parsley, tomato paste, garlic, salt and pepper, and return the mixture to a simmer. Cook the soup for 30 minutes, or until the carrots and potatoes are very tender. Ladle the soup into 4 bowls and sprinkle it with Parmesan.   Makes 4 servings

BAKED POTATO WITH HERBED YOGURT SAUCE

Potatoes, being virtually fat-free and high in complex carbohydrates, are an ideal food for walkers and runners. They are a very good source of vitamin C and potassium, especially when they are baked and the skins are eaten. The herbed yogurt and cottage cheese topping is a satisfying substitute for sour cream or butter.

CALORIES per serving	207
80% Carbohydrate	43 g
17% Protein	9 g
3% Fat	1 g
CALCIUM	119 mg
IRON	4 mg
SODIUM	231 mg

4 large baking potatoes, about
   1/2 pound each
1/2 cup plain lowfat yogurt
1/4 cup lowfat cottage
   cheese (1 %)
1 1/2 cups chopped scallions

1/4 cup chopped fresh parsley
2 tablespoons finely chopped
   fresh chives
1/4 teaspoon salt
1/4 teaspoon white pepper

Preheat the oven to 350° F. Wash and dry the potatoes, then bake them for about 1 hour and 10 minutes, or until they are tender when pierced with a sharp knife. Meanwhile, for the sauce, combine the yogurt, cheese, scallions, parsley, chives, salt and pepper in a medium-size bowl, and stir until well blended; set aside. When the potatoes are done, cut them open and scoop about half of the flesh into a bowl. Mash the potato with a fork, then add it to the bowl of sauce and stir until blended. Divide this mixture among the potatoes, and serve.   Makes 4 servings

Dinner
· · · · · · · · · · · · · · · ·

CHINESE BEEF SAUTE

The iron in beef is better absorbed by the body than that in vegetables. Iron helps make hemoglobin, which carries oxygen to the muscles.

CALORIES per serving	354
68% Carbohydrate	61 g
15% Protein	13 g
17% Fat	7 g
CALCIUM	97 mg
IRON	5 mg
SODIUM	509 mg

1 cup white rice
2 cups thinly sliced carrots
1 tablespoon vegetable oil
1/4 pound lean beef flank steak,
  cut into thin strips
1 red and 1 green bell pepper,
  cut into thin strips
1 1/2 cups chopped scallions
3 garlic cloves, minced

2 cups shredded Chinese cabbage
1/2 pound fresh mushrooms,
  thinly sliced
16 water chestnuts, thinly sliced
3 tablespoons reduced-sodium
  soy sauce
2 tablespoons rice wine vinegar
1 teaspoon sugar
1/4 teaspoon red pepper flakes

Bring 2 cups of water to a boil in a medium-size saucepan over medium-high heat and stir in the rice. Cover the pan, reduce the heat to medium-low and

Chinese Beef Sauté

simmer for 15 minutes, or until the rice is tender and the water is absorbed. Meanwhile, bring a large saucepan of water to a boil. Blanch the carrots in the boiling water for 3 minutes, or until crisp-tender; drain them, cool them under cold running water and set aside to drain thoroughly. When the rice is cooked, remove the pan from the heat and set aside.

Heat the oil in a large nonstick skillet or wok over medium-high heat. Add the beef, and sauté for 3 to 4 minutes, or until browned. Using a slotted spoon, transfer the beef to a small bowl and set aside. Add the bell peppers, scallions and garlic to the skillet and cook, stirring occasionally, for 5 minutes. Add the carrots, cabbage, mushrooms and water chestnuts, increase the heat to high, and cook, stirring frequently, for 5 minutes. Meanwhile, in a small bowl stir together the soy sauce, vinegar, sugar and red pepper flakes. Add this mixture, the rice and the beef to the skillet, and cook, stirring constantly, for 4 to 5 minutes, or until all the ingredients are heated through. Divide the mixture among 4 plates and serve. Makes 4 servings

PESTO PIZZA

This pizza offers a substantial amount of calcium without excessive fat because it is topped with part skim-milk cheese. The vegetables, flour and even the herbs provide some calcium as well. This mineral helps maintain proper muscle function in the heart, lungs and extremities.

1 1/4 teaspoons dry yeast	1/3 cup chopped fresh basil
Pinch of sugar	2 tablespoons grated Parmesan
3/4 cup unbleached all-purpose flour	1 tablespoon chopped walnuts
	1/2 pound red onions
1/4 cup whole-wheat flour	1/2 pound eggplant
1 tablespoon olive oil	3/4 pound tomatoes
1/4 teaspoon plus a pinch of salt	1/2 cup shredded part skim-milk mozzarella
5 large garlic cloves	

CALORIES per serving	262
56% Carbohydrate	38 g
16% Protein	11 g
28% Fat	8 g
CALCIUM	193 mg
IRON	2 mg
SODIUM	294 mg

In a medium-size bowl stir together the yeast, sugar and 6 tablespoons of warm water (105-115° F); set aside for 5 minutes. Add the all-purpose flour, 3 tablespoons of whole-wheat flour, the oil and 1/4 teaspoon of salt, and mix well. Flour the work surface with 1 1/2 teaspoons of whole-wheat flour and knead the dough for 5 minutes. Rinse and dry the bowl. Place the dough in the bowl, cover with a damp kitchen towel and set aside to rise in a draft-free place for 40 minutes, or until doubled in bulk. Meanwhile, for the pesto, bring a small saucepan of water to a boil. Add the garlic cloves, and cook for 5 minutes; peel them and place in a food processor or blender. Add the basil, Parmesan, walnuts, the remaining salt and 1/4 cup of water. Process the mixture for 1 minute, or until thick and smooth; set aside. Peel and trim the onions. Wash and trim the eggplant and tomatoes. Cut the onions, eggplant and tomatoes into thin slices; set aside.

Preheat the oven to 500° F. Punch down the dough. Flour the work surface and a rolling pin with the remaining whole-wheat flour and roll out the dough to a 12-inch round. Transfer it to a pizza pan or baking sheet and crimp the edges of the dough to form a rim. Spread the pesto evenly over the crust and top it with onions, eggplant and tomatoes. Sprinkle the pizza with mozzarella and bake for 15 minutes, or until the cheese is bubbly. Makes 4 servings

ORIENTAL PASTA WITH SNOW PEAS AND PEPPERS

Raw vegetables provide the most vitamins and minerals, but when cooked quickly, by blanching or steaming, they retain most of their nutrients. The broccoli and snow peas provide calcium, while the bell peppers are an excellent source of vitamin C. In fact, a serving of this pasta dish supplies more than twice the recommended daily requirement of this vitamin.

CALORIES per serving	407
74% Carbohydrate	76 g
15% Protein	15 g
11% Fat	5 g
CALCIUM	81 mg
IRON	5 mg
SODIUM	326 mg

1/2 pound snow peas
1 red and 1 yellow bell pepper
2 cups broccoli florets
3/4 pound linguine
1/4 cup low-sodium chicken stock
1 tablespoon vegetable oil

2 tablespoons reduced-sodium
  soy sauce
2 tablespoons lemon juice
2 teaspoons minced fresh ginger
1 garlic clove, minced

Bring a medium-size saucepan of water to a boil. Meanwhile, wash and string the snow peas. Wash, core and coarsely dice the bell peppers; set aside. Blanch the snow peas in the boiling water for 30 seconds, or until they turn bright green. Reserving the boiling water, transfer the snow peas to a colander, cool them under cold running water and set them aside to drain. Blanch the broccoli florets for 3 minutes, or until crisp-tender; cool them and set them aside to drain thoroughly.

Bring a large pot of water to a boil. Cook the linguine in the boiling water for 10 minutes, or according to the package directions, until al dente. Meanwhile, cut the snow peas in half diagonally. For the dressing, combine the stock, oil, soy sauce, lemon juice, ginger and garlic in a small bowl; set aside. Drain the linguine and transfer it to a large serving bowl. Add the snow peas, broccoli, bell peppers and dressing, and toss to combine. Serve immediately.

Makes 4 servings

STUFFED EGGPLANT

If weight control is one of the goals of your exercise program, remember that high-fiber foods help keep you feeling full. This dish provides six grams of dietary fiber per serving.

CALORIES per serving	292
74% Carbohydrate	56 g
16% Protein	12 g
10% Fat	4 g
CALCIUM	176 mg
IRON	4 mg
SODIUM	415 mg

2 small eggplants (about
  1 1/2 pounds total weight)
1/2 pound onions
3 garlic cloves
3 medium-size tomatoes (about
  14 ounces total weight)
1 large red bell pepper
1/4 cup low-sodium chicken stock
1/3 cup chopped fresh parsley

1/2 teaspoon dried thyme
1/2 teaspoon dried oregano
1/2 teaspoon black pepper
1/2 cup skim milk
1 tablespoon chopped walnuts
2 tablespoons grated Parmesan
2 tablespoons wheat germ
1/2 pound Italian bread

Preheat the oven to 350° F. Wash and trim the eggplants and halve them lengthwise. Place the halves cut side down on a foil-lined baking sheet and bake for 30 minutes, or until tender. Meanwhile, peel and coarsely chop the onions and garlic. Wash, core and coarsely dice the tomatoes and bell pepper; set aside.

Leaving the oven at 350° F, remove the eggplant and set it aside to cool slightly. Meanwhile, for the stuffing, heat the stock in a large skillet over medium heat. Add the onions and garlic, and cook, stirring occasionally, for 3 minutes, or until softened. Add the bell pepper, and cook, stirring, for 3 to 4 minutes. Add the tomatoes, parsley, thyme, oregano and 1/4 teaspoon of pepper, and cook, stirring frequently, for 5 minutes more. When the eggplant is cool enough to handle, carefully scoop out and reserve the flesh, leaving a shell about 1/2 inch thick. Coarsely chop the reserved eggplant, add it to the skillet and cook for another 3 minutes. Remove the skillet from the heat and set aside.

For the topping, in a small bowl combine the milk, walnuts, Parmesan, wheat germ and remaining pepper, and stir well. Place the eggplant shells in a baking dish and fill them with the stuffing. Spoon the topping mixture over the stuffing, spreading it evenly. Cover the dish with foil and bake for 30 minutes. Five minutes before the eggplant is done, wrap the bread in foil and place it in the oven to warm. Slice the bread and serve it with the eggplant.

Makes 4 servings

INDIAN CHICKEN WITH POTATOES AND CARROTS

Strong bones are a must for runners, and vitamin A is necessary for proper growth and development of the skeleton. Sweet potatoes are an excellent source of beta carotene, known as the precursor of vitamin A. It is converted to vitamin A only as the body requires it, making it a safer source than vitamin A supplements.

CALORIES per serving	306
64% Carbohydrate	50 g
17% Protein	13 g
19% Fat	7 g
CALCIUM	129 mg
IRON	3 mg
SODIUM	350 mg

1/4 pound skinless, boneless
  chicken breast
1/2 cup plain lowfat yogurt
1 tablespoon lemon juice
1 teaspoon curry powder
1/2 teaspoon ground cumin
1/8 teaspoon Cayenne pepper
1/2 teaspoon salt
1/2 teaspoon black pepper

2 large baking potatoes
  (about 1 pound total weight)
1 large sweet potato
1/2 pound carrots
1/2 pound onions
5 garlic cloves
1 1/2 tablespoons olive oil
1 1/2 tablespoons chopped
  fresh coriander

Cut the chicken into 4 pieces. In a glass bowl stir together the yogurt, lemon juice, curry powder, cumin, Cayenne, 1/4 teaspoon salt and 1/4 teaspoon black pepper. Add the chicken, turning it to coat it evenly with the marinade. Cover the bowl with plastic wrap and let stand at room temperature for 1 hour (or marinate the chicken in the refrigerator for up to 24 hours). Meanwhile, wash and peel the potatoes. Wash and trim the carrots; peel the onions and garlic cloves. Cut the potatoes, carrots and onions into 1-inch chunks; mince the garlic cloves; set aside.

Preheat the oven to 400° F. Combine the vegetables in a large baking dish, sprinkle them with the oil and the remaining salt and pepper, and toss to coat the vegetables with oil. Bake for 30 minutes, or until the potatoes are softened. Add the chicken and marinade to the baking dish and stir to combine. Cover the dish with foil, reduce the oven temperature to 350° F and bake for another 30 minutes, or until the chicken is tender. Transfer the chicken and vegetables to a serving dish, sprinkle with coriander and serve.

Makes 4 servings

Banana-Blueberry Rice Pudding

Dessert

· · · · · · · · · · · · · · ·

BANANA-BLUEBERRY RICE PUDDING

Unlike a dish of premium ice cream, which may contain more than six teaspoons of sugar and 13 grams of fat, this lightly sweetened dessert of fruit and whole grains provides a slow, steady release of carbohydrate energy with a minimum of fat. The rice and bananas are also good sources of potassium and dietary fiber.

CALORIES per serving	224
82% Carbohydrate	48 g
7% Protein	4 g
11% Fat	3 g
CALCIUM	65 mg
IRON	1 mg
SODIUM	45 mg

2 cups cooked brown rice
  (2/3 cup raw)
3/4 cup skim milk
1/4 cup brown sugar
1 tablespoon margarine, melted

1 teaspoon ground cinnamon
3 bananas, peeled and sliced
2 cups fresh or frozen blueberries
1 tablespoon wheat germ

Preheat the oven to 350° F. In a medium-size bowl stir together the rice, milk, sugar, margarine and cinnamon. If using fresh blueberries, wash, dry, stem and pick them over. Gently fold the bananas and blueberries into the rice; transfer it to an 8-inch square baking dish. Sprinkle the pudding with wheat germ, cover it with foil and bake for 30 minutes. Let the pudding cool slightly before serving, then divide it among 6 dessert dishes.   Makes 6 servings

RAISIN-WALNUT BAKED APPLES

Whether part of a well-deserved post-race meal or carried along on a hike, baked apples are a nice change from raw fruit for dessert. Any leftovers make a handy portable breakfast for a busy morning; add the yogurt topping at the last minute.

4 large baking apples, such as
    Rome (about 2 1/4 pounds
    total weight)
2/3 cup dark raisins
1/4 cup coarsely chopped
    walnuts

1/4 cup brown sugar
2 tablespoons freshly squeezed
    lemon juice
1 teaspoon ground cinnamon
1/2 cup plain lowfat yogurt

Preheat the oven to 350° F. Core each apple from the stem end without cutting through the bottom and hollow out a good-size cavity for the filling. Pare a 1-inch strip of peel from the circumference of each apple to prevent splitting during baking; set aside.

    In a small bowl stir together the raisins, walnuts, sugar, 1 tablespoon of lemon juice and the cinnamon. Divide the filling among the apples, then place them in an 8-inch square baking pan. Pour 3 cups of hot tap water into the pan and bake the apples for 1 hour, or until they are very tender; remove them from the oven and set aside to cool slightly. Meanwhile, in a small bowl stir together the yogurt and remaining lemon juice. Top each apple with a dollop of the yogurt mixture and serve. For a portable dessert, wrap the apples while still slightly warm in squares of foil and place them in the refrigerator; refrigerate the yogurt topping in a separate container.   Makes 4 servings

CALORIES per serving	332
81% Carbohydrate	73 g
4% Protein	4 g
15% Fat	6 g
CALCIUM	106 mg
IRON	2 mg
SODIUM	28 mg

RASPBERRY BREAD PUDDING

Basing a dessert on bread, skim milk and fruit makes for a treat with a variety of nutritional advantages. Italian bread is extremely low in fat; skim milk is one of the best sources of dietary calcium (none of the mineral is lost when the fat is removed); and the raspberries are an excellent source of vitamin C and provide almost four grams of dietary fiber in a serving of this dessert.

1/2 pound Italian bread
2 1/4 cups skim milk
1/3 cup brown sugar
2 eggs

1 teaspoon ground cinnamon
1 teaspoon vanilla extract
3 cups fresh or frozen raspberries

CALORIES per serving	242
75% Carbohydrate	45 g
15% Protein	9 g
10% Fat	3 g
CALCIUM	157 mg
IRON	2 mg
SODIUM	296 mg

Cut the bread into 1-inch cubes and place them in a large bowl. Combine the milk, sugar, eggs, cinnamon and vanilla in a medium-size bowl and whisk until well blended. Pour the milk mixture over the bread, add the raspberries, and toss gently to combine. Transfer the mixture to an 8-inch round baking dish and cover it with a plate that will rest on top of the pudding. Place a weight (such as a heavy can or a package of dried beans) on the plate and set aside at room temperature for 30 minutes.

    Preheat the oven to 350° F. Remove the weight and the plate, cover the baking dish with foil and bake the pudding for 30 minutes. Serve it warm or at room temperature.   Makes 6 servings

Creamy Cantaloupe Soda

Snacks and Beverages

CREAMY CANTALOUPE SODA

It is preferable to get carbohydrates from fruits and fruit juices than from the added refined sugar—up to ten teaspoons—in a can of soda.

CALORIES per serving	82
80% Carbohydrate	17 g
12% Protein	3 g
8% Fat	1 g
CALCIUM	68 mg
IRON	.4 mg
SODIUM	34 mg

One cantaloupe (about 2 pounds)
1/2 cup plain lowfat yogurt
1 cup seltzer

3 tablespoons frozen
   apple-juice concentrate
Ice cubes (optional)

Using a melon baller or a spoon, scoop the cantaloupe into a medium-size bowl; you should have about 3 cups. Combine the cantaloupe, yogurt, seltzer and apple-juice concentrate in a blender and process on high speed for about 1 minute, or until thick and smooth. Pour the soda into 4 tall glasses, over ice if desired, and serve.

Makes 4 servings

CARIBBEAN SHAKE

Keeping your body well hydrated helps ensure the proper functioning of your muscles. Drink lots of water during exercise, and enjoy this cool tropical-fruit shake afterward.

One 20-ounce can juice-packed
  crushed pineapple, drained
1 banana, peeled and sliced
1 cup skim milk

1 cup ice cubes
1/2 teaspoon coconut extract
4 mint sprigs

CALORIES per serving	133
90% Carbohydrate	32 g
8% Protein	3 g
2% Fat	.4 g
CALCIUM	97 mg
IRON	.5 mg
SODIUM	34 mg

In a blender combine the pineapple, banana, milk, ice cubes and coconut extract. Blend on high speed for 2 minutes, or until thick and smooth. Pour the shake into 4 tall glasses, garnish with mint sprigs and serve.

Makes 4 servings

ONION-CURRY FLATBREAD

In order to maintain a high energy level, replenish your body's glycogen stores by eating carbohydrates within two hours of exercising. A generous slice of this flatbread will provide 38 grams of carbohydrates.

1 tablespoon light brown sugar
1 package dry yeast
3 cups whole-wheat flour
1 1/2 cups unbleached all-purpose
  flour, approximately
1/2 pound red onions
4 garlic cloves

2 tablespoons olive oil
1 teaspoon curry powder
1/4 teaspoon salt
1/4 teaspoon black pepper
Vegetable cooking spray
1 egg

CALORIES per serving	204
71% Carbohydrate	38 g
13% Protein	7 g
16% Fat	4 g
CALCIUM	27 mg
IRON	2 mg
SODIUM	53 mg

In a large bowl stir together the sugar, yeast and 1 1/4 cups of warm water (105-115° F); set aside for 10 minutes. Stir in the whole-wheat flour, then add about 1 1/4 cups of all-purpose flour, or enough to form a soft dough. Turn the dough out onto a lightly floured surface and knead it for 10 minutes, kneading in additional all-purpose flour as necessary to make the dough smooth and elastic. Rinse and dry the bowl. Form the dough into a ball, place it in the bowl, cover it with a damp kitchen towel and set aside to rise in a draft-free place for 1 to 1 1/2 hours, or until doubled in bulk.

While the dough rises, peel the onions and garlic. Thinly slice the onions and mince the garlic. Heat the oil in a large skillet over medium heat. Add the onions, garlic, curry powder, salt and pepper, and cook, stirring frequently, for 7 minutes, or until the onions are softened. Remove the pan from the heat and set aside.

Preheat the oven to 450° F. Lightly spray 2 large baking sheets with cooking spray. Break the egg into a small bowl and beat it until blended; set aside. Punch down the dough and divide it into 6 equal pieces; cover them with a kitchen towel. Place 1 piece of dough on a lightly floured board and roll it out to an 8 x 5-inch rectangle, leaving the edges slightly thicker than the center. Transfer this piece of dough to a baking sheet and brush it with egg, then top it with onions and garlic. Repeat with the remaining dough. Bake the flatbreads for 15 minutes, or until lightly browned. Let cool slightly before serving. Cut the breads in half and serve.

Makes 12 servings

PROP CREDITS

Cover: tank top and shorts–The Finals, Port Jervis, N.Y., running shoes–Avia, Alexandria, Va.; page 6: woman's tank top–The Finals, Port Jervis, N.Y., running shoes–Nike, Inc., Beaverton, Ore.; pages 24-25: woman's hiking boots–Eastern Mountain Sports, New York City, Air Trainers High shoes–Nike, Inc., Beaverton, Ore., running shoes courtesy of Athletic Style, New York City, Air Walkers Plus shoes–Nike, Inc., courtesy of Athletic Style, New York City; pages 26-27: backpack, fanny pack, water bottle and compass–Eastern Mountain Sports, New York City, watch–The Finals, Port Jervis, N.Y.; page 28: walking shorts–Naturalife, New York City, walking shoes–Avia, Alexandria, Va.; pages 34-43: walking shoes–Avia, Alexandria, Va.; pages 46-49: tank top–The Finals, Port Jervis, N.Y.; page 52: hiking boots–Nike, Inc., Beaverton, Ore., shorts–Patagonia, Ventura, Calif., long-sleeve T-shirt–Naturalife, New York City; pages 54-59: hiking boots–Nike, Inc., Beaverton, Ore.; page 60: tank top, shorts and running shoes–Nike, Inc., Beaverton, Ore.; pages 66-69: shorts–The Finals, Port Jervis, N.Y., running shoes–Avia, Alexandria, Va.; pages 70-75: tank top–The Finals, Port Jervis, N.Y., shorts–Nike, Inc., Beaverton, Ore., running shoes–Avia, Alexandria, Va.; pages 76-81: shorts–The Finals, Port Jervis, N.Y., running shoes–Avia, Alexandria, Va.; pages 82-89: man's shorts and woman's tank top–The Finals, Port Jervis, N.Y., woman's shorts–Nike, Inc., Beaverton, Ore., running shoes–Avia, Alexandria, Va.; page 90: running clothes–The Finals, Port Jervis, N.Y., Nike, Inc., Beaverton, Ore., running shoes–Avia, Alexandria, Va.; page 92: tank top–The Finals, Port Jervis, N.Y., shorts–Nike, Inc., Beaverton, Ore., running shoes–Avia, Alexandria, Va.; page 93: shorts–The Finals, Port Jervis, N.Y., running shoes–Avia, Alexandria, Va.; pages 116-123: shoes–Avia, Alexandria, Va.; page 128: flatware, tea service, plate and fruit bowl–Sasaki, New York City, basket–Gear Stores, New York City; page 131: plate–Gear Stores, New York City.

ACKNOWLEDGMENTS

Our thanks to Kent Ohlund

All cosmetics and grooming products supplied by Clinique Labs, Inc., New York City

Nutrition analysis provided by Hill Nutrition Associates, Fayetteville, N.Y.

Off-camera warm-up equipment: rowing machine supplied by Precor USA, Redmond, Wash.; Tunturi stationary bicycle supplied by Amerec Corp., Bellevue, Wash.

Washing machine and dryer supplied by White-Westinghouse, Columbus, Ohio

Index prepared by Robert Hernandez

Production by Giga Communications

PHOTOGRAPHY CREDITS

Exercise photographs ©David Madison 1988, except photographs on pages 94-95 ©Nancie Battaglia 1985; pages 98-99 ©DUOMO/Steven E. Sutton 1985; pages 100-103 ©Warren Morgan; page 104 by John Iacono/Sports Illustrated; Food photographs and equipment on pages 24-27 by Steven Mays, Rebus, Inc.

ILLUSTRATION CREDITS

Pages 9, 33, illustrations: Phil Scheuer; pages 10, 13, 18-19, 20-21, 22-23, 106-107, charts: Brian Sisco; pages 15, 44-45, 50-51, 78-79, illustrations: David Flaherty

Time-Life Books Inc. offers a wide range of fine recordings, including a Rock 'n' Roll Era *series. For subscription information, call 1-800-621-7026, or write TIME-LIFE MUSIC, P. O. Box C-32068; Richmond, Virginia 23261-2068.*

INDEX

National Institutes of Health,
  recommendations of, 127
neuroma, 23
north, magnetic, 27, 57

Oblique muscles, 123
Olympic athletes, 32
Olympics, Seoul, 32
orienteering, 18, 30, 31, 54-59
osteoporosis, 8, 127
oxygen consumption, 8, 15, 18, 94

Pace, 17, 18, 87, 92, 99
  jogging, 65
  maintaining, 101
partners, training with, 50, 83-89
  see also fartlek training; games, partner
passing, 89
pasta, 132
Peachtree Road Race, 62, 64
petroleum jelly, 96
posture
  in running, 65
  in walking, 38, 44, 109, 111
potassium, 130, 133, 138
prancing, 80
President's Council on Physical Fitness, 62
progressive resistance exercise, 111
pronation, excessive, 24
protein
  amounts in recipe dishes, 128-141
  metabolism, 125
  primary function of, 125
  recommended intake of, 127
psychotherapy, and running, 62
pullovers, 112

Race walking, 18, 31-32, 46-51, 110
  errors, 50-51
  Olympic, 32
  rules for competition, 46
  technique, 32
raise, lateral arm, 116
recipes, 128-141
  beverage, 140-141
  breakfast, 128-130
  dessert, 138-139

dinner, 134-137
lunch, 131-133
snack, 140-141
recovery rate, 64, 92, 105
repetitions, exercise, 110-111
reps, see repetitions
road racing, 14, 94
routines
  running, 20-21
  upper body, 112-123
  walking, 18-19
rows, bent-over, 113
running
  biomechanical action of, 9, 62
  cardiovascular benefits of, 61-62
  efficiency of, 30
  injuries, 22-23, 62, 63, 64
  intervals, 63, 92-93
  pace, 101
  psychological benefits of, 8, 61-62, 83
  stretches for, 66-69
  stride, 70-73
  technical mistakes, 78-79
  training for, 20-21, 106-107
  with a partner, 83-89
  workouts, 20-21
sciatica, 23
shin splints, 23, 44
shoes, 17, 24, 64, 96
shoulder muscles, 114, 116-117
shoulder swings, 110, 112
shrugs, shoulder, 117
side bends, lateral, 123
single-arm raise, 117
sit-ups, 122-123
slow-twitch muscle fibers, 110-111
slumping, 44
snack recipes, 140
sodium
  amounts in recipe dishes, 128-141
  restriction of intake of, 125-127
specificity, principle of, 110
speed play, 14, 65
  see also fartlek training
sprinters, 110
sprinting, 75, 80, 89, 105
stairs, climbing, 31
stopwatch, 27, 94
stress test, 13, 16
stretches, 34-37, 66-69

stride, foot, 110
  see also running, walking
sucrose, 126
sugar, simple, 126
Swedish Olympic Team, 65

Tag, playing while running, 83
target heart rate, 10, 12, 17, 30, 43, 45
ten-K race, 63, 94
training effect, 15
trapezius muscles, 117
treadmill, running, 12, 16, 65
triceps muscles, 114, 119
triglycerides, 8
  see also cholesterol

Upper back muscles, 112

Vegetables, raw, 136
vertical lift, 110
VO_2max, 11, 12, 17, 61, 125

Walk-a-thons, 32
Walkers Club of America, 32
walking
  aerobic benefits of, 30
  biomechanics of, 9, 30, 38
  common mistakes, 44-45
  efficiency, 29-30
  foot placement, 33
  increasing the effort of, 19, 42-43
  routines, 18-19
  stride, 18, 29, 33, 38-41
  warm-ups and stretches for, 34-37
  see also race walking
warm-ups, 30, 111
water bottles, 91
weight control, 8, 12, 14, 16, 62, 127, 136
weight shifts, 110
weight training, 109-123
  see also progressive resistance exercise
windmills, exercise, 37
wobblies, 32

Yogurt, lowfat, 133, 139